MUSIC A
SECONDARY

Miguel Ángel López Ballester
José Palazón Herrera
José Luis Salas Martínez
Raquel Cavas Hernández

Pedagogical Advisor
Inmaculada Martínez Riazuelo

Mc Graw Hill Education
MADRID · BUENOS AIRES · CARACAS · GUATEMALA · LISBON
MEXICO · NEW YORK · PANAMA · SAN JUAN · BOGOTÁ · SÃO PAULO
AUCKLAND · HAMBURG · LONDON · MILAN · MONTREAL · NEW DELHI · PARIS
SAN FRANCISCO · SYDNEY · SINGAPORE · SAINT LOUIS · TOKYO · TORONTO

CONTENTS

HOW TO USE THIS BOOK

Unit Introduction

Go to the Online Learning Centre to download the accompanying worksheets for this section.

Here are the topics we are going to study.

Before you begin, there are warm-up activities to introduce the key concepts for each unit.

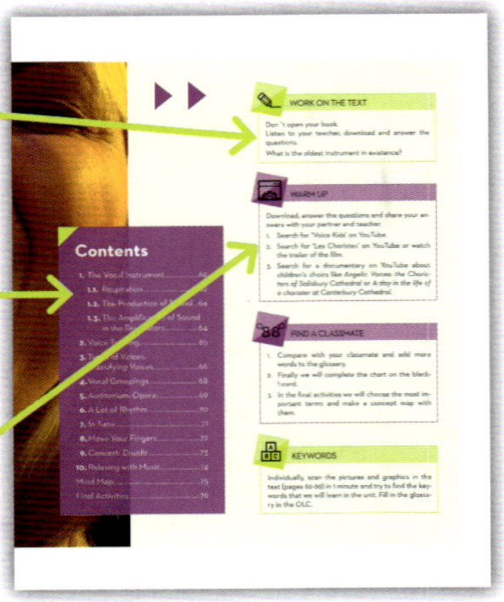

Content development

PRACTICAL EXERCISES

The exercises give you the opportunity to put the music theory and music history into practice using instruments and your voice.

ACTIVITIES

Progressive learning activities to work on the contents as they are explained.

SYMBOLS

Clear and concise explanations of the theory accompanied by information blocks to help you understand the most important points.

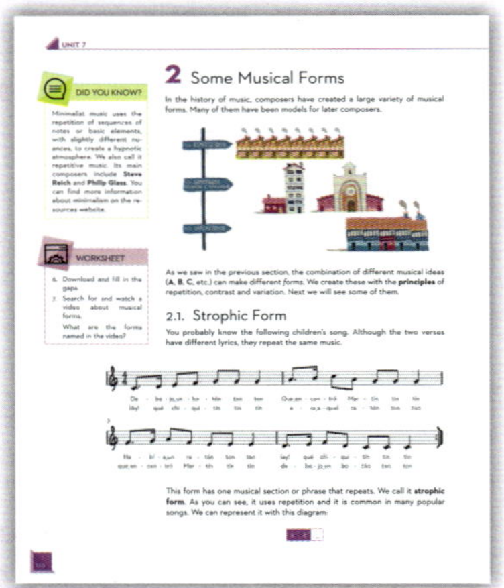

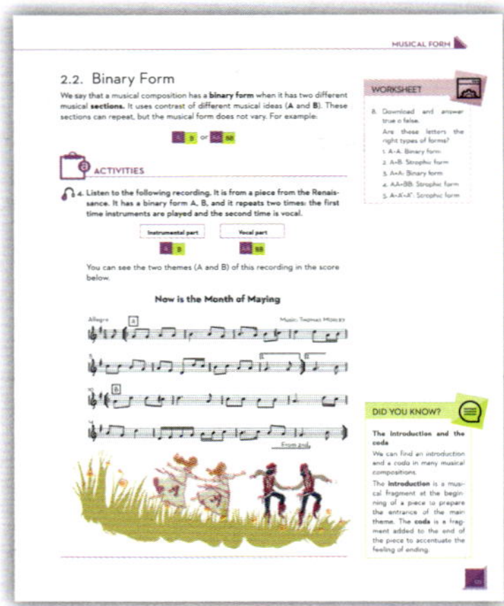

DID YOU KNOW?

RESOURCES WEB

CURIOUS FACTS

REMEMBER

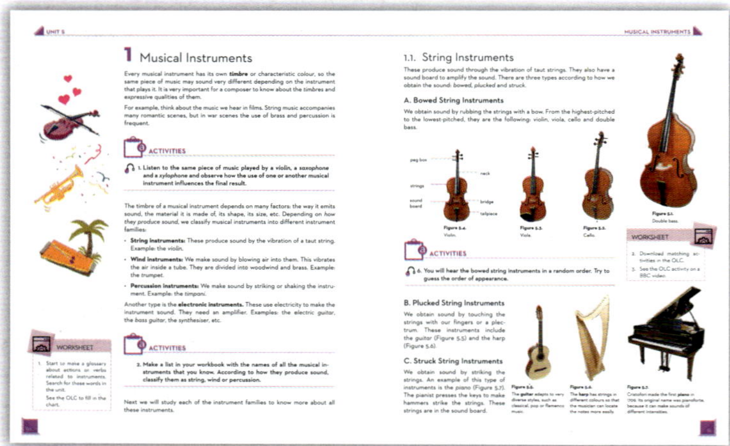

WORKSHEET

Each unit has complementary activities distributed by headings. Download the worksheets from the Online Learning Centre.

RESOURCES WEB

Remember, throughout the unit we recommend you visit the OLC and download the worksheets associated with the content of each unit.

www.mheducation.es

OLC STUDENT

End of Unit

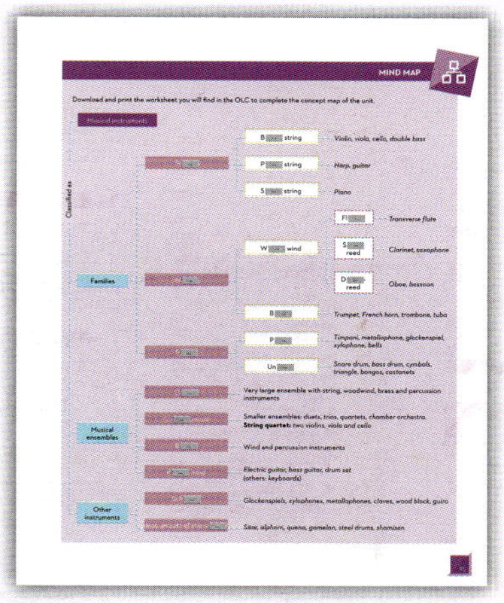

MIND MAP

A review of the basic concepts you have learned in each unit.

FINAL ACTIVITIES

Individual and group exercises to check your learning progress.

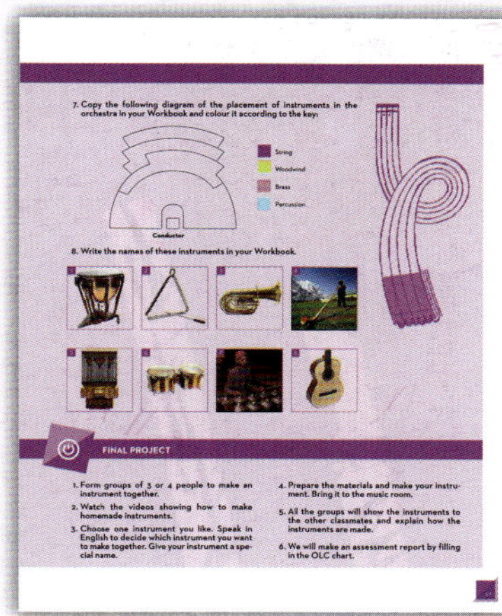

FINAL PROJECT

Group projects which require planning, searching for information, data analysis, and the organisation and presentation of information.

Recordings

Each unit has a specific resource section with numerous illustrative recordings. These are examples of the book content so you can study, practise and understand the material.

TEACHING BOOK

Teacher's available videos.

Complementary material

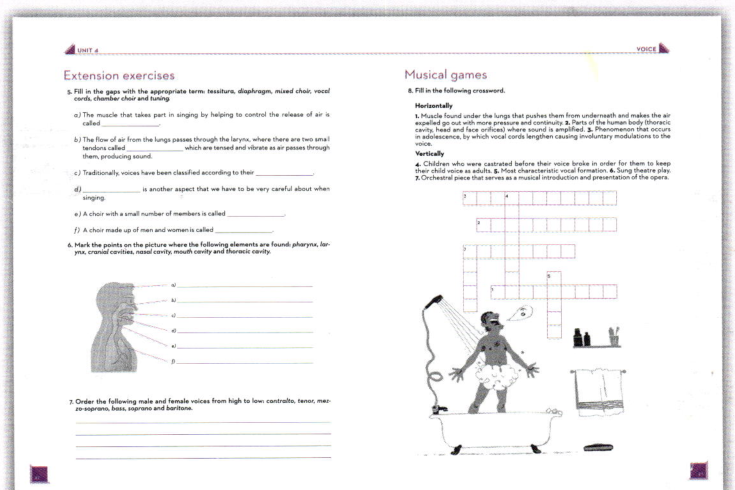

Music A - Secondary is not just the student text book. To help you study, we have included some **complementary materials.**

WORKBOOK

You can do all the activities included in the course in your Workbook. The Workbook also includes extra activities to help you consolidate or increase your knowledge of various aspects of each unit.

1 THE QUALITIES OF SOUND

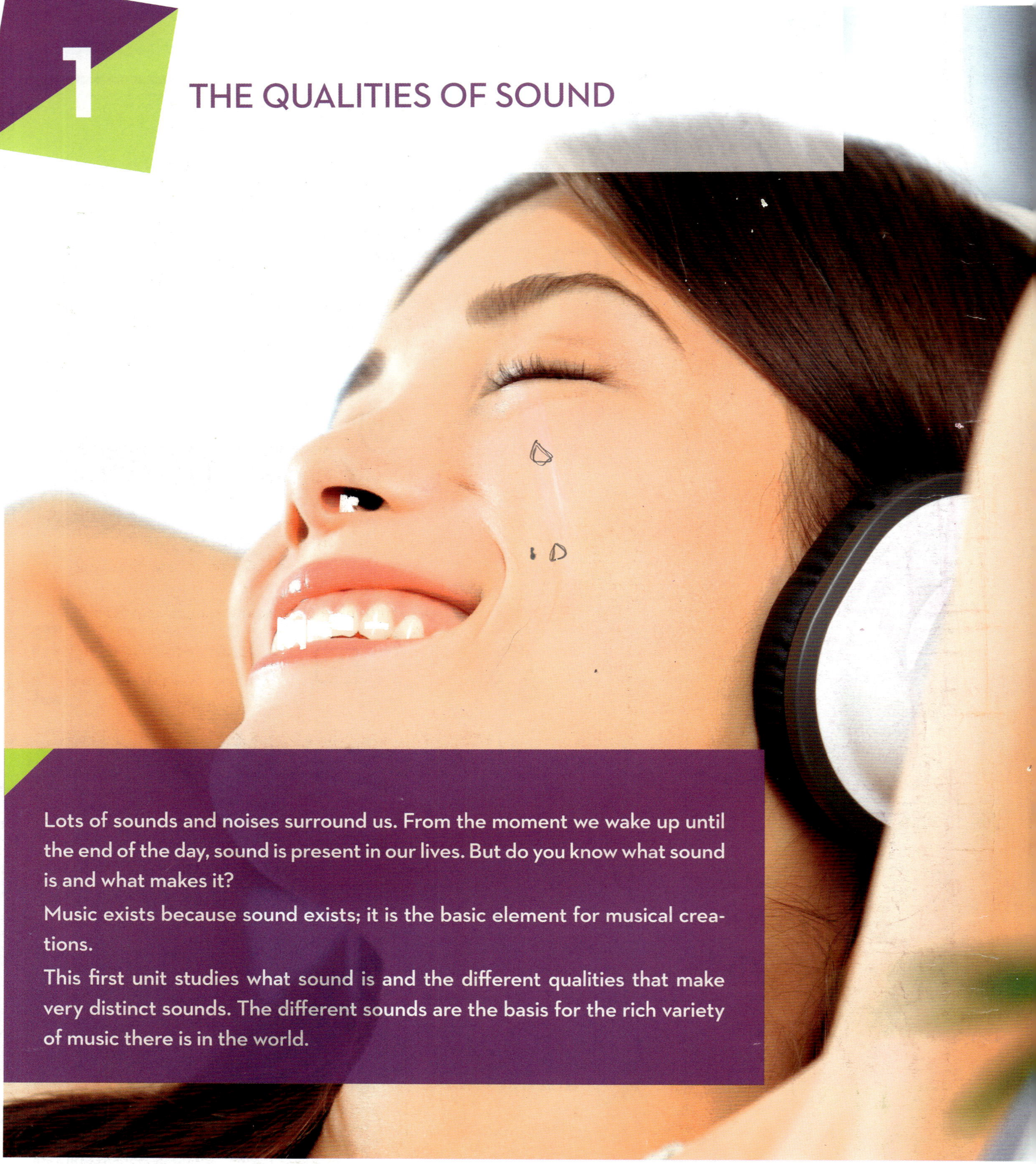

Lots of sounds and noises surround us. From the moment we wake up until the end of the day, sound is present in our lives. But do you know what sound is and what makes it?

Music exists because sound exists; it is the basic element for musical creations.

This first unit studies what sound is and the different qualities that make very distinct sounds. The different sounds are the basis for the rich variety of music there is in the world.

Contents

WORK ON THE TEXT

Download the worksheet 'Work on the text' and fill in the gaps in the activity.

1. Sound is present in our l ...
2. There is a variety of music in the world. Sound is the b ...
   The basic element for music creation is s ...
3. We are going to study:
   a) ... sound is
   b) The different q ... of sound.

WARM UP

Answer these questions:

1. What is the material to make music?
2. Do you think 'sound' and 'noise' are the same thing? Why?
3. Do you think that 'absolute silence' is possible? Why?

FIND A CLASSMATE

1. Share your individual answers with your partner and then share with your group.
2. A spokesperson representative of the groups, will explain your conclusions to the class.

KEYWORDS

Download and print the activities that will guide you through the essential vocabulary of this unit.

1 Sound, Noise and Silence

1.1. Sound

Figure 1.1.
Image of a drop falling into water, producing waves.

Music is essentially sound. Just as a sculptor uses stone and other materials to create works of art, a composer manipulates and orders sound to make music.

We are always surrounded by sound, but do you know what sound is and what makes it?

Sound is produced when an object vibrates. When you strum the strings on a guitar, they begin to vibrate and make sound. The same thing happens when you bang a drum: its membrane vibrates and produces sound.

The vibrations are transmitted in the form of sound waves. These waves travel through different media: air, water, wood, etc. Think about what happens when you throw a stone into water. The stone makes the water vibrate and produces ripples (Figure 1.1). These ripples are similar to sound waves moving through the air.

WORKSHEET

1. Put the words in the right order:
   brain / sound waves /auditory canal / eardrum / auditory nerve.
2. Read this page and fill in the glossary.

ACTIVITIES

1. **Sound travels in sound waves, but you cannot see them. Do you want to prove this?**
   Make a tuning fork vibrate and put the base against your elbow. Now put your finger in your ear. Can you hear anything? If you can, it is because the bones in your arm transmit the sound.

We perceive these waves through our ears (Figure 1.2). They have an elastic membrane called the eardrum. This membrane vibrates when sound waves reach it. This information then travels to the brain. The sensation we perceive is sound.

RESOURCES WEB

You can find information about tuning forks on the website.

To sum up, sound is the sensation we experience when sound waves reach our ears. The vibrations from a sonorous object make the sound waves.

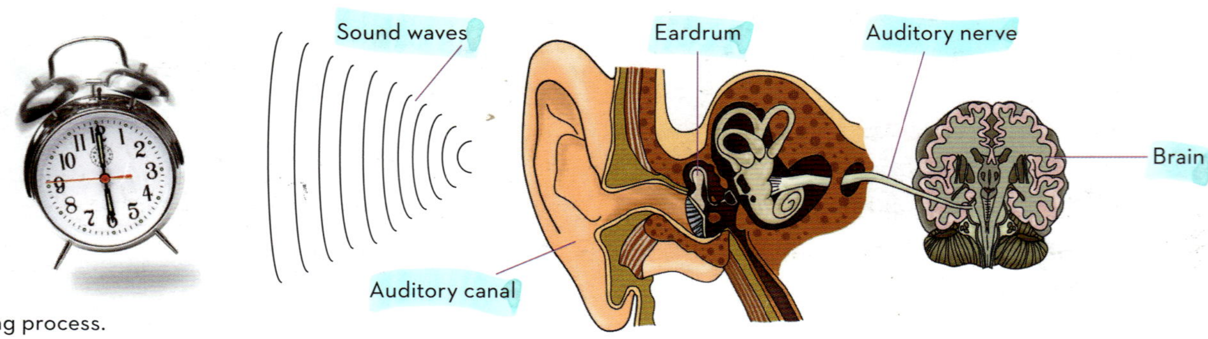

Figure 1.2.
Diagram of the hearing process.

1.2. Noise

What is the difference between sound and *noise*?

Noise is usually defined as something that sounds bad, but this definition is subjective and imprecise. Most percussion instruments produce noise when they are played, but they sound good to our ears.

We can use a physical definition to distinguish between noise and sound. Look at the waves in the following diagrams:

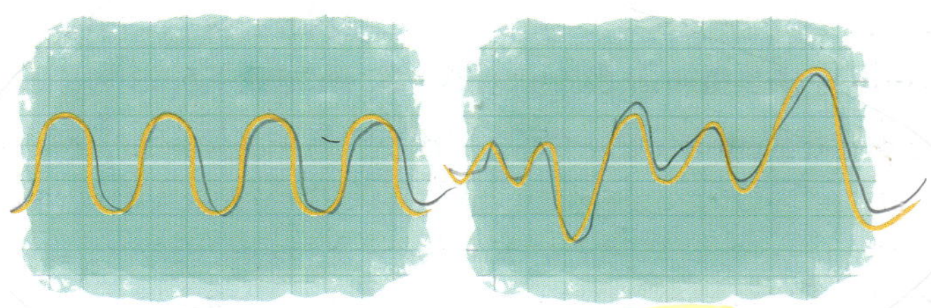

As you can see from the first diagram, the wave of a **sound** is *regular*. However, in the graph for **noise**, the wave is *irregular*.

We say there is **noise pollution** when the acoustic levels are very high. This is a new problem for our society, as it affects our quality of life and has a harmful effect on our health.

Some sources of noise pollution are: different types of transport, industrial activity, construction, nightclubs, bars, etc.

Noise can affect our health in many ways. For example, it can make communication difficult or interrupt our sleep. It can also cause stress, aggressive behaviour, cardiovascular and digestive diseases or even a partial loss of hearing.

WORKSHEET

3. Make a mind map with the following words:
   - Music
   - Hearing process
   - Sound
   - Silence
   - Noise
4. Read this page with your teacher and fill in the glossary.

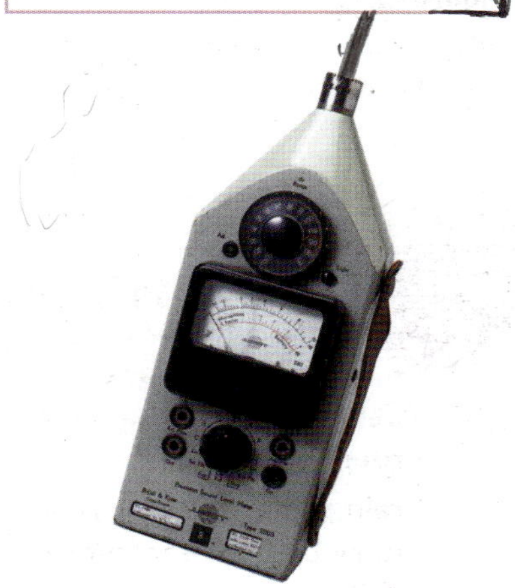

Figure 1.3.
The level of noise is measured in decibels (dB). The apparatus used to measure noise is called a **sound level meter.**

ACTIVITIES

2. Listen to the next track or 'sound passage'. Write in your Workbook all the noises and musical sounds you can identify. Can you invent a story based on what you heard?

3. Write in your Workbook a description of all the sounds and noises you hear around you on a normal day. Do you think there is noise pollution in your surroundings? Use the table on the right to help you with your answer.

WHO (World Health Organisation) says that the acceptable noise limit is an average of 65 dB per day (Figure 1.3).

Finally, think about possible solutions to reduce the noise levels around us.

Birds singing	10 dB
Leaves moving on the trees	20 dB
Normal conversation	50 dB
Traffic	85 dB
Inside nightclubs	110 dB
Motorbikes without silencers	115 dB
A plane flying	130 dB

WORKSHEET

5. Watch the videos and complete the activities.
6. Read this page and fill in the glossary.
7. Download the pdfs on the WHO website about 'Make Listening Safe' to know how to take care of your hearing.

1.3. Silence

Silence is the absence of sound or noise.

The combined use of sound and silence is the basis for musical creation.

Some composers use silence as a main component in their creations. One example of this technique is the work 4'33" by the composer **John Cage**. The performer goes on stage and maintains absolute silence for the time indicated in the title. However, there are noises and sounds from the audience and in the concert hall. The audience are the true protagonists of the piece.

Another example is the *String Quartet* by **G. Bridit**. For this piece, four instrumentalists walk on stage, shake hands, remain silent for a while, and then leave the stage.

DID YOU KNOW?

Recent studies by audiology experts show that the continuous use of MP3 players at high volume produces irreversible hearing loss in many youngsters.

ACTIVITIES

4. With your voice (and other musical instruments or objects) make random sounds or noises. When your teacher gives you the signal, stop suddenly. Repeat the exercise two or three times and evaluate the positive effect of silence. Tell your classmate, group or teacher.

CURIOUS FACTS

Does absolute silence exist?

The American composer **John Cage** conducted an experiment to check whether absolute silence exists or not. He went inside an **anechoic chamber** or soundproofed room (Figure 1.4).

He concluded that absolute silence does not exist, because he heard two sounds inside the chamber. One was a low sound (his blood flowing inside his body) and the other was a high sound (his nervous system functioning).

Silence is the absence of sound and noise. Some composers use silence

2 The Qualities of Sound and Their Graphic Representation

You have learned what sound is, but not all sounds are the same. They have different characteristics, as we will see below.

WORKSHEET

8. You can play different games with your teacher's help.
9. Read pages 11-14 and fill in the glossary.

ACTIVITIES

5. **Using a metallophone (Figure 1.5), try to make two sounds that are as different from each other as possible. Clues:**
   - They should be distant from one another.
   - One should last longer than the other.
   - Play one with greater force than the other.

   Now repeat the two sounds, but play one of them on the xylophone (Figure 1.6).

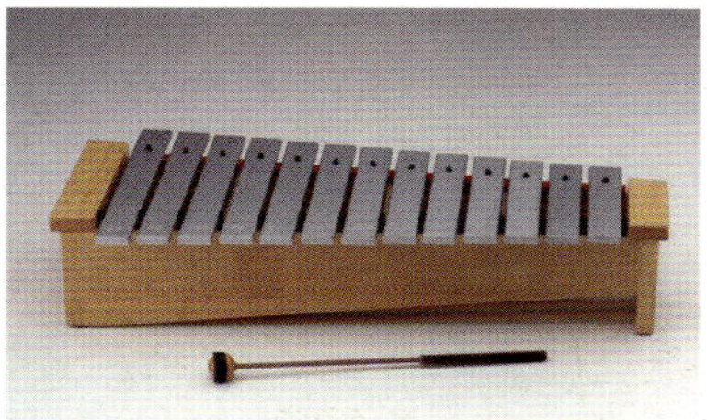

Figure 1.5.
Metallophone. Instrument with metal bars.

Figure 1.6.
Xylophone. Instrument with wooden bars.

In the previous activity you noticed that:

- When you play towards the right of the instrument (on the smaller bars), the sound is progressively higher. When you move towards the left, it becomes lower. In this case, there is a variation in the quality of sound called **pitch**. Pitch lets us classify sounds as *low*, *medium* or *high*.
- If you use the mallet to hit the instrument harder, you make a louder sound. If you hit it more gently, the sound is softer. The quality of sound that varies is the **dynamic intensity**. The dynamics let us classify sounds as *loud*, *medium loud* and *soft*.
- The sounds on the metallophone last for longer than those you played on the xylophone. This is the quality of sound we call **duration**. This lets us classify sounds as *short* or *long*.
- Did you hear the difference in sound when you play two different instruments (the xylophone and the metallophone)? This 'tone colour' is called **timbre**. The timbre gives each instrument and voice its unique sound. It means we can identify which instrument is playing or whose voice is singing.

ACTIVITIES

6. **Listen to the following tracks and say which sound quality predominates over the others.**
   a) *Autumn* (1st Movement): **Vivaldi**
   b) *Goyescas* (Intermezzo): **Granados**
   c) *Scheherazade*: **Rimsky-Korsakov**
   d) *The Young Person's Guide to the Orchestra*: **Britten**

WORKSHEET

10. Find among the words below:
    a) Words related to PITCH.
    b) Words not related to PITCH:
    long, low, loud, high, short, soft, clef, stave, minim, crochet, rest.

As you have heard, sound has different **qualities** or parameters. These qualities help us to classify the differences in the music we hear.

Sound qualities	Distinction between the sounds
Pitch	High / Low
Duration	Long / Short
Dynamic intensity	Loud / Soft
Timbre	Voices and instruments

2.1. Pitch grave/agudo

Pitch is the quality of sound which makes a distinction between *low* and *high* sounds.

RESOURCES WEB

You can find more information on the acoustic indices on the website.

ACTIVITIES

7. **Classify the pitch of the following sounds as low, medium or high.**

The following musical notes represent the pitch of sounds:

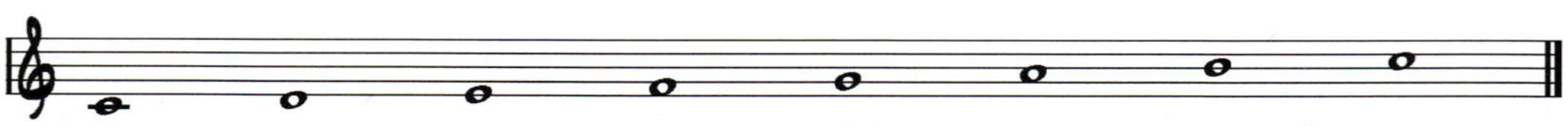

C D E F G A B C

REMEMBER

Stave: the set of five lines and four spaces on which we write music.

Clef: the musical symbol which identifies the pitch of the notes.

G

ACTIVITIES

8. **Circle the lowest note in each pair of sounds.**

2.2. Duration (Duracion)

Duration is the quality which differentiates between long and short sounds.

ACTIVITIES

9. Listen to the following sounds played by your teacher. Copy the boxes below into your Workbook and note the duration of each sound. Each box represents one beat. Example:

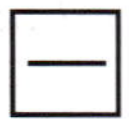

Sound lasting 1 beat

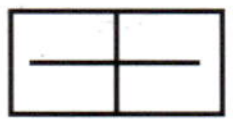

Sound lasting 2 beats

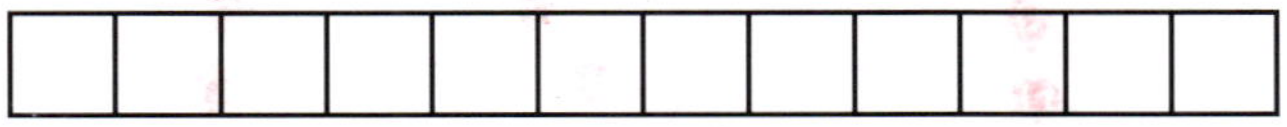

Note values and rests represent the duration of sounds:

semibreve	minim	crotchet	quaver	semiquaver

4	2	1	1/2	1/4

ACTIVITIES

10. In your Workbook translate the durations of the previous activity into note values.

WORKSHEET

11. Find among the words below:
    a) Terms related to DURATION.
    b) Terms not related to DURATION:

    long, low, loud, high, short, soft, clef, stave, minim, crochet, note, note value.

DID YOU KNOW?

Repetition symbols are used to avoid rewriting the fragments which are repeated in the score. You studied some of them in previous classes. Here is a reminder of the most important ones:

Repeat bars

Repeat from the start.

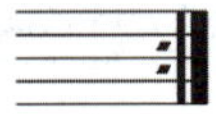

Repeat the fragment contained between the two bars.

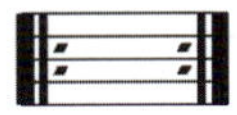

Time signature: It tells you how many and what kind of notes per measure there are. The number on top is the number of notes per measure, and the bottom number is the kind of note counted in the measure.

2.3. Dynamic Intensity

The **dynamic intensity** is the quality that distinguishes between *loud* and *soft* sounds.

ACTIVITIES

11. Your teacher will interpret a series of rhythms with different intensities. Listen carefully and repeat them.

Dynamic markings represent the intensity of sound:

pp	***p***	***mf***	***f***	***ff***
pianissimo	*piano*	*mezzo-forte*	*forte*	*fortissimo*
(very soft)	(soft)	(medium)	(loud)	(very loud)

crescendo (increasingly loud)

diminuendo (increasingly soft)

ACTIVITIES

12. Clap your hands to interpret this sequence of 16 beats. Try to respect the dynamic intensity indications as much as possible.

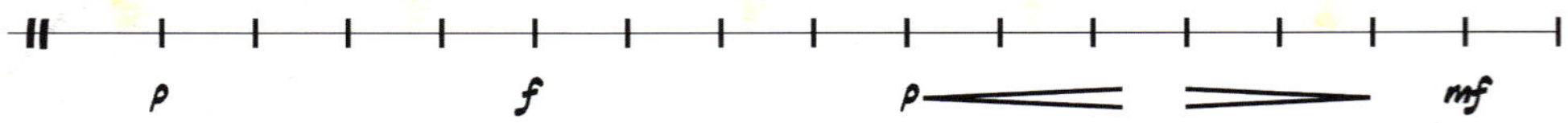

WORKSHEET

12. Find among the words below:
    a) Terms related to DYNAMICS.
    b) Terms not related to DYNAMICS.

    long, forte, low, piano, loud, high, short, soft, clef, stave, minim, crochet, crescendo, note, note value, dynamic markings.

2.4. Timbre

Timbre is the quality of sound which indicates who or what is producing it.

This is how we can tell what type of voice or instrument it is just by listening to it.

ACTIVITIES

13. Listen to the recording and identify how many changes of timbre occur.

3 Auditorium: Music in Film

A. The Soundtrack

You probably go to the cinema to watch films sometimes. What do you think it would be like to watch a film without any music in it? Can you imagine a horror film, a Western or an action movie without music?

We often use the word *soundtrack* to refer to the music in a film, but it is more than that.

The **soundtrack** actually means all the sound which accompanies the images on screen: the music, the sound effects and the dialogue.

Music in film adds realism and depth to a scene, a character or a situation. Let us examine some examples of famous sounds and melodies from some important genres of film.

Figure 1.7.
Scene from the film *Psycho*, directed by Alfred Hitchcock. Search for the Psycho shower scene on the internet.

B. The Music

Music in film is so varied that it is impossible to summarise everything in this small space. So let us take a brief look at some very significant genres:

The dissonant, threatening sounds of the string instruments in **Alfred Hitchcock**'s *Psycho* (Figure 1.7), with music by **Bernard Herrmann.**

The famous melody with a 'heroic' tone (performed by a wind, metal and percussion section) from the theme song to the *Indiana Jones* films (Figure 1.8). The director was **Steven Spielberg** and **John Williams** composed the music.

Sergio Leone's *The Good, the Bad and the Ugly*, with music by **Ennio Morricone**. This film has the most whistled melody in the history of cinema and one of the most representative tunes from the Western genre.

In the film *Blade Runner* (directed by **Ridley Scott**), the composer **Vangelis** uses electronic sounds (synthesisers and others) to reflect a futuristic world. In this world there are robots known as 'replicants' and they are as intelligent as the engineers who created them. Vangelis is also famous for his music for *Chariots of Fire*.

Figure 1.8.
Poster from the film *Indiana Jones and the Kingdom of the Crystal Skull*. Search for the Indiana Jones theme song on the internet.

4 A Lot of Rhythm

In this first lesson we will work on the beat. The beat is the internal rhythm of the music and serves as a guide when you play an instrument or sing.

1. Listen to this sequence. It contains various rhythmic patterns. Notice how all the patterns have a common beat.
2. Follow this diagram of 16 beats and mark the beats you hear in the exercise with an X. Before you begin, you will hear four introductory beats.

3. Listen to this fragment of classical music with a beat in the background. The beat will come and go. Try to keep marking the beat even when you cannot hear it and see if you synchronise with it when it reappears.
4. Now let us work with the internal beat. Clap along only to the marked beats. Follow the other ones in your head (without marking them with any part of your body). Did your claps coincide with all the ones you heard? Congratulations! You have good internal rhythm.

Remember that the exercise begins after the first four introductory beats.

WORKSHEET

13. Read the page and fill in the glossary.
14. See the glossary: useful expressions in regard to rhythm.

DID YOU KNOW?

Music can provoke changes in your heartbeat. This is because your emotions change when your hear music and your heart rate accelerates or decelerates.

5 In Tune

Do you want to sing better? In this section you will learn how to use and tune your voice. You will also learn how to read scores. Then you can sing along to your favourite songs with a better voice!

> **DID YOU KNOW?**
>
> Lots of the singers you listen to have singing coaches. They help singers to improve their voice and keep it in good form through exercises. These exercises are similar to the ones you are doing here.

A. Train Your Voice

Just as your body gets strong by doing exercise, you can also strengthen and train your voice by practising exercises called **vocalisations**. You will learn how to do some of these to help improve your vocal abilities.

The following exercise is a good starting point to pitch your voice correctly. You can practise it using the background included on the unit resources.

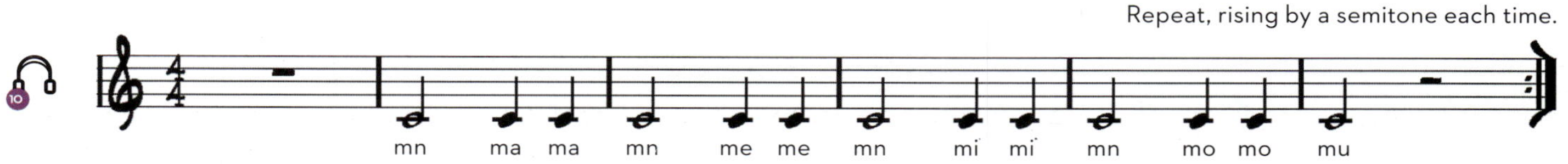

B. Reading Music

Reading music on a stave is very important. It is quite easy, but first you must practise every day to learn how to do it well.

We are going to study the first three notes in the major scale: the notes *C*, *D* and *E*. Mark a beat and try to read each of the notes in the following fragment. Read them silently in your head, without singing.

> **WORKSHEET**
>
> 15. Read the page and fill in the glossary.

C. Interpretative Exercise

Now practise singing the following score over a musical background. At the beginning you will hear 4 introductory beats and the note C. This will help you to tune your voice correctly before singing.

> **WORKSHEET**
>
> 16. See the glossary: useful expressions in regard to singing.

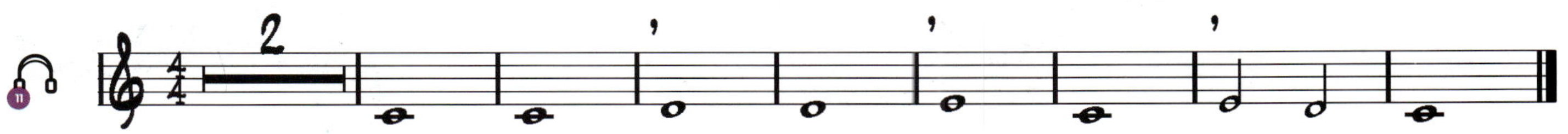

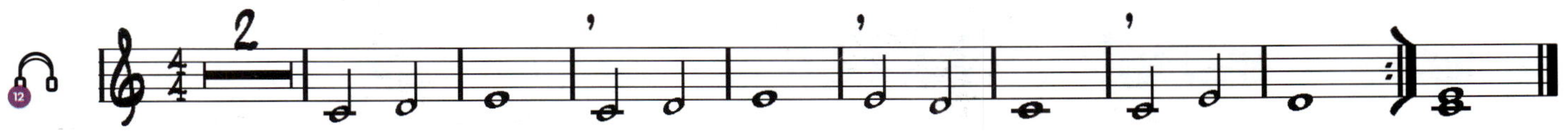

6 Move Your Fingers

You are going to play the following exercises on your **recorders.** Your teacher will use signals to help you, using the accompaniment on the unit resources.

If you have any doubts about the finger positions on the recorder, look at the appendix on pages 174 to 175.

We are going to use the following accompaniments for these exercises:

- For Exercises 1, 2 and 3, we will use a background created with electronic instruments and drums.
- For Exercises 4, 5 and 6, we will use a different background with a classical style. The instruments you will hear are the *double bass*, the *cello* and *violins*.

All right, you are ready to play the exercises below. Enjoy them!

WORKSHEET

17. See the glossary: useful expressions in regard to playing the recorder.

Exercise 1 *B-A G*

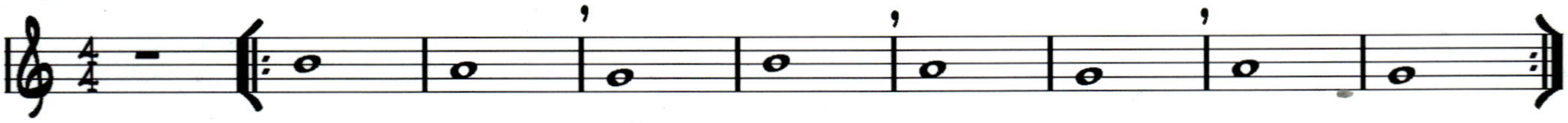

Exercise 2

Exercise 3

Exercise 4

Exercise 5

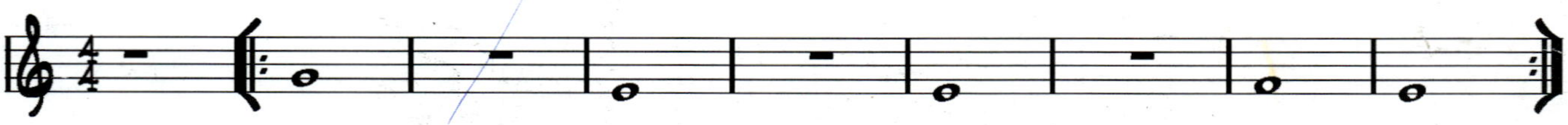

Exercise 6

7 Concert

Welcome to our *Concert* section. In this first unit, we are going to play the symphony piece *Pangea* on the recorder or **keyboard percussion instruments.** The piece is in the style of the **great soundtracks.** You learned a little about this important genre in the *Auditorium* section.

With the help of your teacher, you will learn this simple piece step by step. Then we will play it together with the sound of an entire symphony orchestra (Figure 1.10).

D

Figure 1.9.
Finger position on the recorder for the note *D.*

Pangea

Music: José Luis Salas

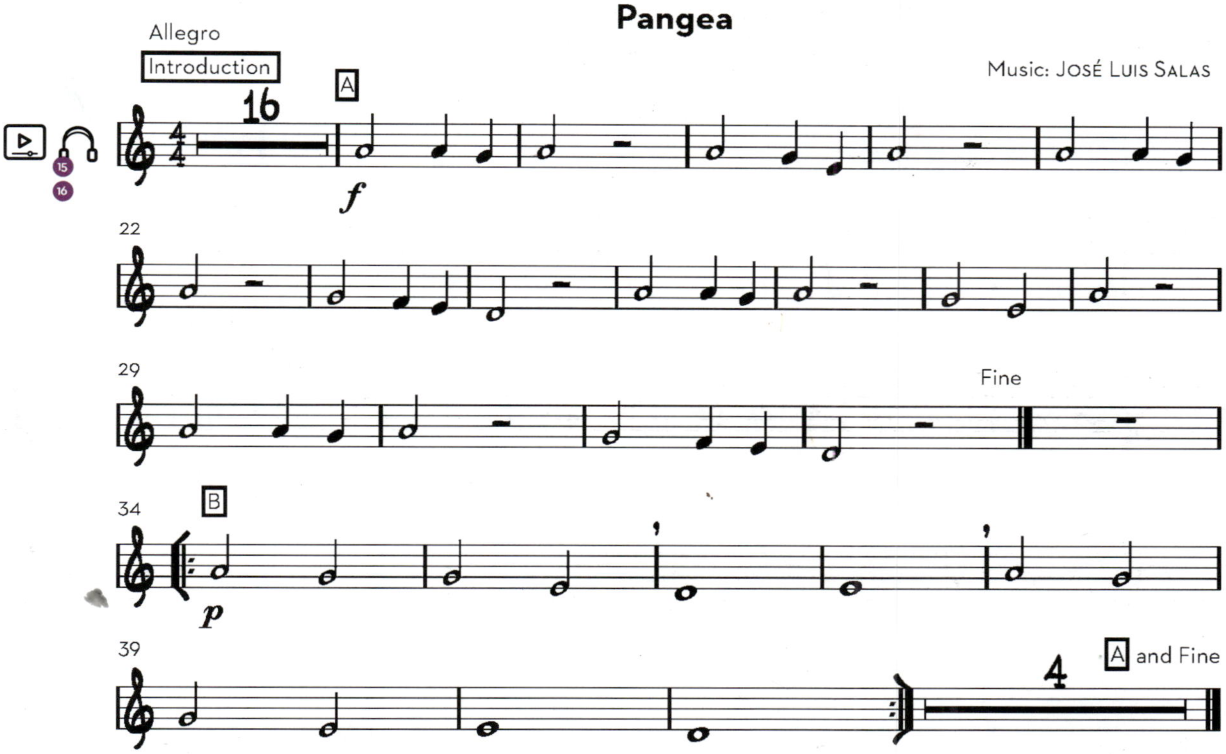

WORKSHEET

18. Read pages 18-19 and fill in the glossary.

Figure 1.10.
A symphony orchestra is a large musical group with all the families of instruments.

Now try to play a composition called *Cosmos* on your recorder. The piece has the style of a soundtrack and includes elements of electronic music. Try to create a beautiful, intense journey towards a distant galaxy. It should be easy to play because it uses the same notes you practised in *Pangea*.

Cosmos

Music: José Luis Salas

Download and print the worksheet you will find in the OLC to complete the concept map of the unit.

S …	The s … we experience when the w … produced by the *regular* v … of a s … object reach our e … s.
N …	Produced by the *i* … *vibration* of a s … body.
S …	The a … of sound or n …

The qualities of s …

	Description:	Represented by:
Pitch	H … / L …	S …, clef and musical n …
Duration	L … / S …	Note v … and rests
Dynamic Intensity	L … / S …	Dynamic m …
Timbre	Who or w … is emitting the sound	Voices or i …

M … notation

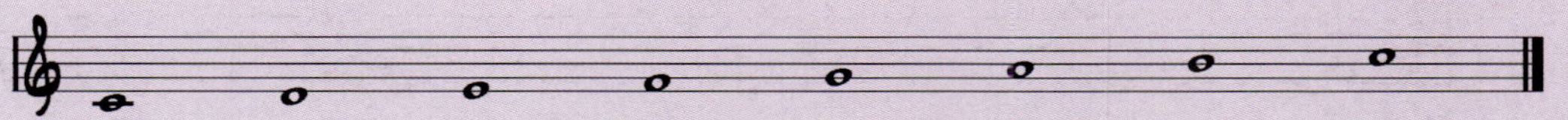

C D E F G A B C

N … v … and rests

s …	m …	c …	q …	s …

4	…	…	1/2	1/4

Dynamic m …

pp	*p*	*mf*	*f*	*ff*	*crescendo*	*diminuendo*
p … (very soft)	*p* … (s …)	*m* … (medium)	*f* … (loud)	*f* … (very …)	(i … loud)	(i … soft)

FINAL ACTIVITIES

1. Use the recorder or the keyboard percussion instruments to make pairs of sounds with the following qualities:

a) 1. Loud/Short; 2. Soft/Long.

b) 1. Long/Low; 2. Short/High.

c) 1. Long/Soft; 2. Short/Loud.

2. Experiment with your voice:

a) Sing a loud sound and change to a soft sound without interruption.

b) Sing a low sound and change to a high sound without interruption.

3. In your Workbook match the following qualities to their characteristics:

Pitch •	• Loud/Soft
Duration •	• Long/Short
Dynamic intensity •	• Voice/Instrument
Timbre •	• High/Low

4. Listen to the following sequence of sounds played by your teacher. For each sound, write down the qualities of sound you hear. All the qualities have a medium point. They can be high, medium or low; long, medium long or short; soft, medium loud or loud.

	Pitch	Duration	Dynamics
Sound 1	...	...	...
Sound 2	...	...	...
Sound 3	...	...	...
Sound 4	...	...	...

5. Click on the link to watch an animation about the effects of noise on the body: http://www.andaluciainvestiga.com/espanol/cienciaAnimada/sites/ruido/ruido.swf. Use it to answer the following questions:

a) Current legislation sets a decibel limit for noise. Above this limit, noise has a harmful effect. What is the decibel limit?

Name a noise above this limit. Now name a noise above the pain threshold.

b) Name three physiological effects that noise can have on people.

6. **Complete the following sentences in your Workbook using words related to sound qualities:**

a) The parameter or quality of time is the ... .

b) A loud or soft sound is indicated by the ... .

c) That voice sounds familiar, I recognise its ... .

d) Her voice was so ... that I couldn't hear her.

e) The siren made a very ... sound.

f) The speakers were so ... that my ears rang for days.

7. **Look at the score below. Copy it into your Workbook and write the correct name below each note:**

8. **Copy the following table into your Workbook. Write the name and duration next to each note value. Draw the symbols for the rests.**

	Name	Duration	Rest	Spanish	American
𝅝	...	...	...	...	...
𝅗𝅥	...	...	...	...	...
♩	...	...	...	...	...
♪	...	...	...	...	...
𝅘𝅥𝅯	...	...	...	...	...

FINAL PROJECT

In groups of 4 or 5 pupils

1. Make a set of cards based on the English version of the OLC chart 'Qualities of sound'.
2. Be creative with shapes, colours and techniques. You can make the graphics by hand or with your computer (for example with Paint or with other online apps) but include the main terms you have studied in the Unit.
3. If you want you can use an old set of cards as a template to stick your drawings on.
4. When you finish your set (or while you are working on it), think about different games you know. Then write the instructions in English with your teacher's help.
5. Every group shows the others how to play with their set of cards.
6. Your group plays the other classmates' games.
7. Your teacher will assess your work: cards, instructions and knowledge of the qualities of sound.

2 RHYTHM

Rhythm is one of the most important elements in music. Some people call it the 'engine of music'.

But rhythm is not exclusive to music. It exists in nature too. For example, the Earth revolves around the Sun every 24 hours and the seasons come and go each year. Our bodies also have natural rhythms: our heartbeat, our breathing, and so on.

Rhythm is present in language, in theatre and in film (scenic rhythm), and it is the base of dance.

In this unit we will study the concept of rhythm and learn how it is represented. We will read and play different rhythms. In short, we are going to experiment with rhythm.

Contents

WORK ON THE TEXT

Read with your teacher, download the worksheet and fill in the gaps.

1. R ... is: one of the most important e ... in music. Present in n ... in our b ... in language, in t ... and in f ... . It is also in the base of d ... .
2. In this unit we are going to study the c ... of rhythm and how it is r ... . We'll r ... and p ... different rhythms and ex ... with them ... .

WARM UP

1. Search on the internet for a video by the group Stomp or Mayumana. Watch it. Download, fill in the gaps or answer the questions.
2. Download the worksheet and listen to the work 'The rite of spring'.
   a) What kind of music is it? What do you think is the most important musical element in this piece: melody or rhythm?
   b) Is this calm classical music?
   c) Can you say the composer of this piece?
   d) What date was the work called 'La ...' in Spanish composed?
   e) It was composed in ... and when it was first performed it was a sensation.

FIND A CLASSMATE

Download the worksheet: Which video/music do you prefer and why?

KEYWORDS

Download and print the activities that will guide you through the essential vocabulary of this unit.

WORKSHEET

1. Put the following groups of words in the right order to make a definition of BEAT:

   of music /constant / in all types / pulse / the regular / present.

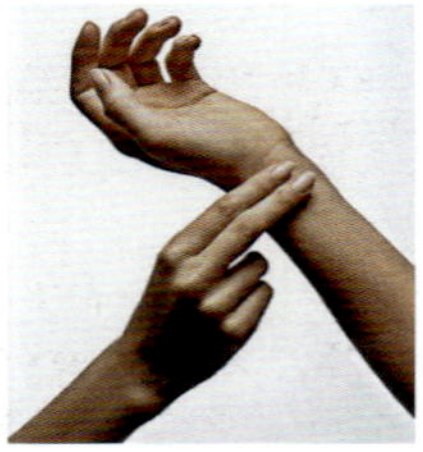

Figure 2.1.

A person is taking someone's pulse. This is the beat inside our bodies.

1 Beat and Tempo

1.1. Beat

When you listen to a song, you probably move your head or tap your foot in time to the music. This is marking the *beat* (Figure 2.1).

However, a beat is not exclusive to music. There are lots of examples: your heart marks the rhythm of your blood; a tap dripping water; a clock ticking, etc.

A musical **beat** is the regular, constant pulse present in all types of music.

In the *A Lot of Rhythm* section in Unit 1, you learnt a little about the beat. Let's look at it in more depth.

You will learn how important the beat is in any form of musical expression: dance, reading music, playing music, and so on. Can you think about the beat every time you listen to music? Let's see.

ACTIVITIES

1. **Listen to the following recordings. You will hear the beat in each one. Observe that:**
   - The beat in both fragments is regular and constant.
   - The speed of the beat is different in the two recordings.
   - Although the two examples are from different musical styles, they both have a beat.

2. **Mark the beat of the following recordings by tapping your finger on the table.**

   Do you want to check your internal beat? Your teacher will lower the volume of the recording. You will not hear it for a few seconds. Keep marking the beat at the same speed. Then the volume will increase again. Did you keep the beat?

3. **Mark the beat by walking (or tapping your feet if you are sitting). Imagine that you are doing *crotchets*. At the same time, clap your hands marking *crotchets*. Then clap *minims*. Finally, mark *quavers* with your hands. Follow your teacher's signals.**

4. **Make the rhythmic series by clapping or by tapping your hands on the table. Pay special attention to the *rests*, but continue marking the beat in your head.**

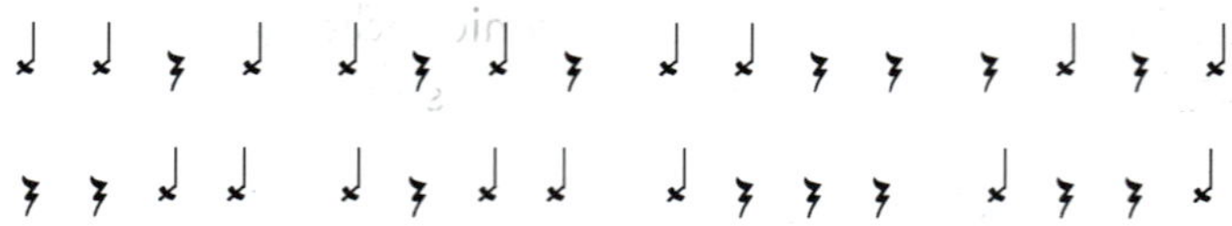

   Repeat the exercise at different speeds.

5. **Play with numbers.**

   Your teacher will mark a constant beat. At the same time he/she will show you a number with his/her fingers. Count out loud, saying 'One,' 'One-two,' 'One-two-three' or 'One-two-three-four,' depending on the number of fingers your teacher holds up.

1.2. Tempo

As you saw in Activity 4, one fragment of music can be played at different speeds.

> The speed of the beat is called the **tempo.**

We use some special Italian words to indicate the tempo of a piece of music. Here are some of the most commonly used terms.

Indications for *tempo*

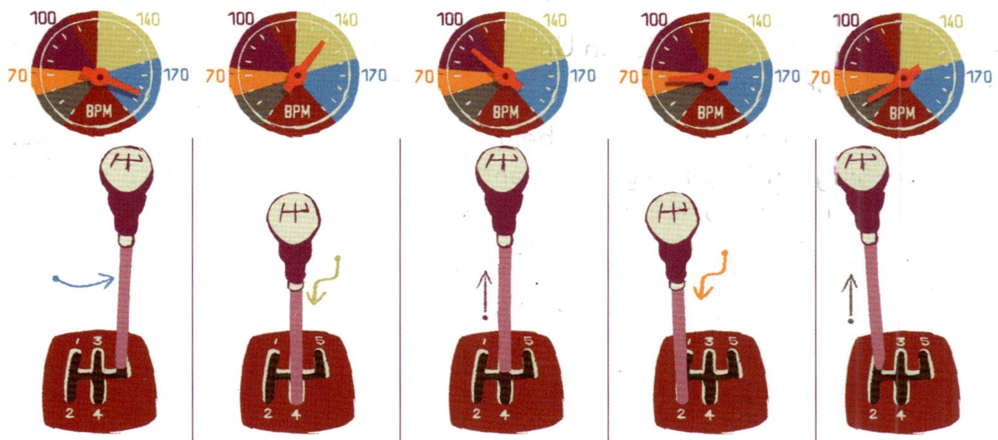

Presto Very fast | ***Allegro*** Fast | ***Andante*** Medium | ***Adagio*** Slow | ***Largo*** Very slow

Accelerando (acc.) Increasingly faster

Ritardando (rit.) Increasingly slower

The indications for tempo are not exact. Two different pianists will play a piece for the piano marked allegro at different speeds. To help musicians play at the same speed, we use metronomic indications (Figure 2.2). For example, the indication ♩ = **120** means that the speed is 120 beats per minute.

ACTIVITIES

6. **Listen to the recordings from Activity 2 again. In your Workbook, match the three fragments to their corresponding *tempo*.**

Fragment 1 •	• *Presto*
Fragment 2 •	• *Allegro*
Fragment 3 •	• *Adagio*

DID YOU KNOW?

Italian is the universal language of music. This means that it does not matter where musicians are from or what language they speak. Anyone who can read music can understand the musical terms.

WORKSHEET

2. Put the following terms in order from slowest to fastest: Adagio / Largo / Presto / Andante / Allegro.
3. Visit the website and do the activity about Tempo.
4. Watch the video 'How Rhythm Works' (part 1) and fill in the sentences.

Figure 2.2.

Image of a metronome. Musicians use a device called a metronome to measure the speed of the beat.

Do you want to test your rhythm? Play a song you know on the recorder and use the metronome.

Use the online metronome: http://simple.bestmetronome.com/

WORKSHEET

5. Download and answer the questions: Can you pronounce 3 words you choose emphasising their syllables?

   How many syllables are there in every word?

   Share the words with your partner.
6. You can also do the OLC activities about 'meter' and 'measure'.

2 Accent and Meter

The beat by itself is neutral. This means that all the pulsations are equal, with no differences between them. However, all music has implicit *accents* or *stresses*.

The same thing happens with language. We emphasise some syllables more than others. The pattern of *accents* in the beats of music is called meter.

Example of neutral beat	| | | | | | | | | | | |
	> > >
Example of accented beats	| | | | | | | | | | | |

In the second example there is a regular accentuation (every four beats).

The **meter** organises the accents in a series of beats into a regular pattern. Depending on how these accents are distributed, we have different types of meters. Every group of beats is a measure or a bar.

Duple:
accent every two beats

>   >
\| \| \| \|
1 2 1 2

Triple:
accent every three beats

>   >
\| \| \| \| \| \|
1 2 3 1 2 3

Quadruple:
accent every four beats

>   >
\| \| \| \| \| \| \| \|
1 2 3 4 1 2 3 4

Some musical styles always use the same type of meter. For example, the *merengue* is a Latin dance and it uses the duple meter. A well-known ballroom dance called the *waltz* is in triple meter. However, most of the music you usually hear on the radio (*pop, rock,* etc.) uses quadruple meter.

ACTIVITIES

7. Practise the different types of meters above. Divide the class into two groups. The first group has to mark the beat and the second group marks only the accented beats. Follow the accents of the meter your teacher indicates.

8. Hum a well-known song marking the beat and finding its accentuation. Try this with melodies you know.

9. Listen to the following recordings. Listen for the accent every few beats and try to guess the meter.

WORKSHEET

7. Download and choose the right answer about time signatures.
   Say an example to your partner of time signature and swap examples.
8. Make the domino of rhythm and play.

Meters are represented by **time signatures** or fractions (Figure 2.3):

The *numerator* indicates the number of beats each **measure** or **bar** has.

$\frac{2}{4}$	$\frac{3}{4}$	$\frac{4}{4}$
2 beats	3 beats	4 beats

The *denominator* indicates the length of the beats. In music each note value is associated to a number. A whole note (semibreve) can be divided into different note values. The number comes from these **note values.**

A semibreve is equal to two minims, four crotchets, eight quavers or sixteen semiquavers. The following diagram illustrates the equivalences between the different note values.

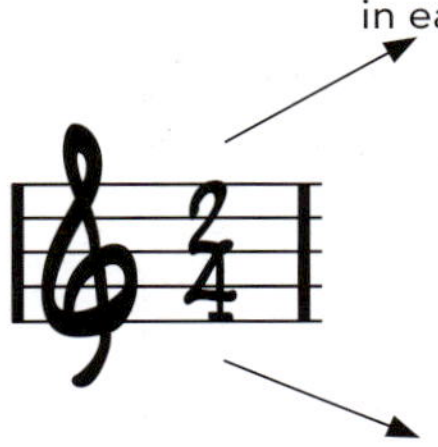

Figure 2.3.
Time signature to represent the meter. The image shows a 2/4 meter.

Note value equivalence table

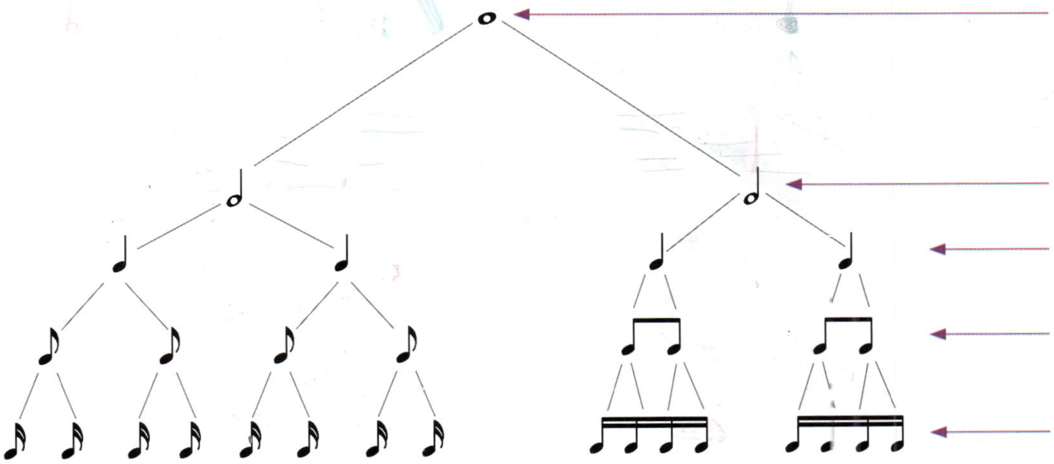

REMEMBER

- The line used to separate measures is called the **bar line.**

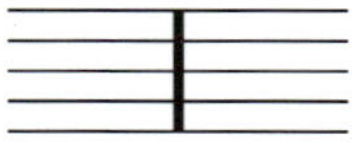

- The **bold double bar line** is at the end of the sheet music. It tells us where a piece of music finishes.

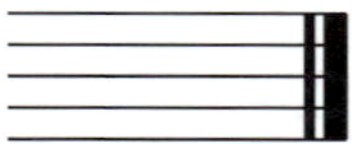

Note that the crotchet is identified with the number 4, because a semibreve is equal to 4 crotchets. In the three previous meters the denominator is 4. So, the length of the beat is the crotchet.

Duple meter

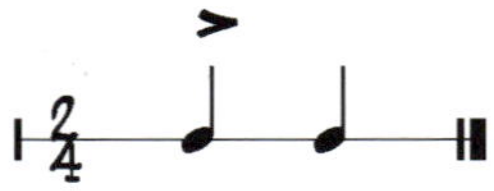

Triple meter

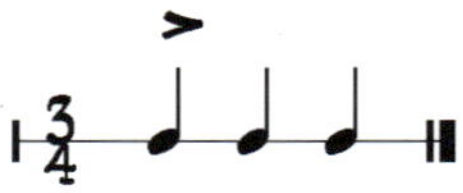

Quadruple meter

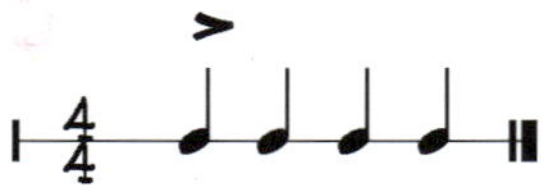

Using the equivalences between the note values, we can find multiple combinations of meters in the same measure. For example:

ACTIVITIES

10. Resolve the following exercises:

a) In your Workbook, complete the following equivalences with the correct note value:

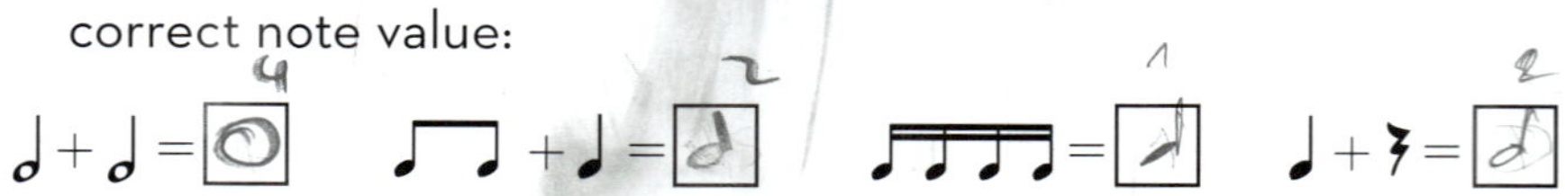

b) Put bar lines in the correct places:

c) Complete the measures with the correct note values:

d) Complete the measures with the correct rests:

WORKSHEET

9. Download and fill in the gaps.
   - Answer and swap other similar questions with your partner.
     How many minims are there in a semibreve?
     How many crotchets are there in a minim?
     How many quavers are there in a semibreve? And in a crotchet?

3 Rhythm

We often hear expressions such as 'Dancing to the rhythm of life' or 'Look how well he dances; he's got great rhythm!' But can you define what rhythm is? Maybe it is difficult, but you can probably play or invent a *rhythm*. Try this example:

In Section 1 of this unit, we saw that the beat is a constant, regular pulse. The rest of the music develops around it. However, there are combinations of sounds with different durations in all music.

Rhythm can be defined as the combination of sounds with different durations that flow around a beat.

ACTIVITIES

11. Repeat the rhythm above, but this time mark the beat with your foot at the same time.

12. Let's listen to **Steven Adler,** the drummer from **Guns N' Roses** (Figure 2.4). He played one of their greatest hits: the very famous Paradise City. First mark the beat to the song. Now listen again. This time, try to play the rhythm made by the drums. Finally, split the class into two groups. One of them will mark the beat and the other will play the rhythm.

WORKSHEET

10. Download and fill in the gaps.
11. See an example of a jumbled definition in the OLC.

Figure 2.4.
A concert by the rock band **Guns N' Roses.**

Rhythm has existed since the beginning of ages. However, note values and meter were invented by musicians to represent rhythm in a graphic form.

WORKSHEET

12. Watch the video from the film 'El milagro de Candeal'. Listen carefully to learn how to create a polyrhythm. You can try the same in your group.
13. Watch the video 'How Rhythm Works' and fill in the gaps.

ACTIVITIES

13. Play the following rhythms. They use the same combination of note values, but observe how they change when we use a different meter.

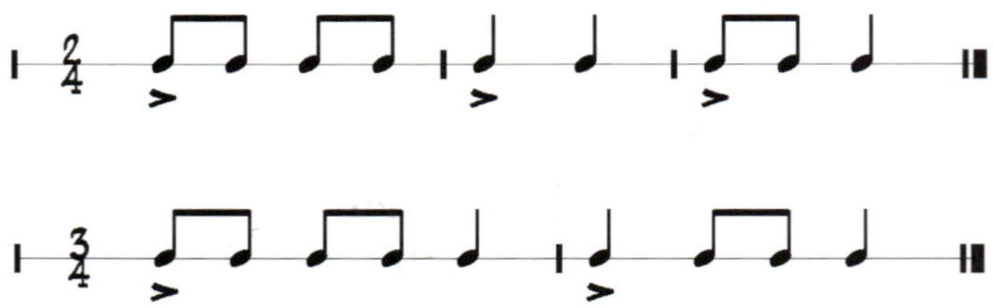

14. Some rhythms seem very familiar to us. Try to associate the following examples with the correct word:

a)

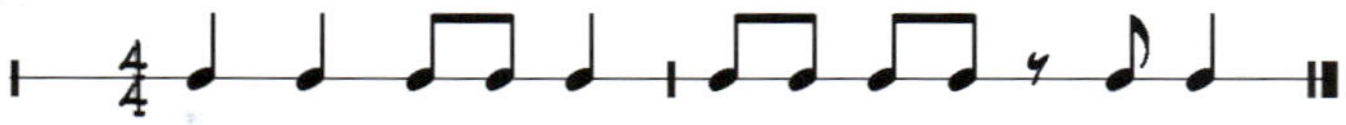

b)

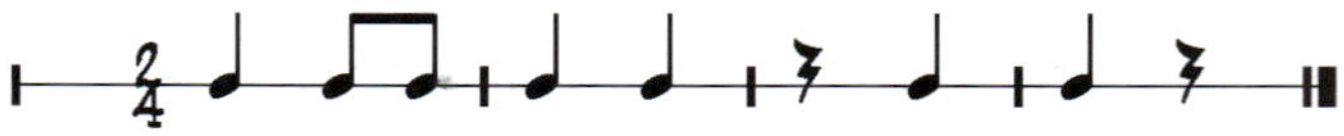

- Meals
- Sports
- The end of something
- Films

15. We usually associate rhythm with percussion instruments. But we must not forget that melodies have rhythm too. You are going to listen to the well-known melody *A Little Night Music* by Mozart. First you will just hear the rhythm. Then you will hear the melody. Finally, you will hear both parts at the same time.

16. Now think of a famous song and try to hum the melody and clap the rhythm.

When we play various rhythms simultaneously, it creates a **polyrhythm.**

In some cultures we find very rich rhythms and highly complex polyrhythms (Figure 2.5).

Figure 2.5.
African music has a rich rhythmic base.

ACTIVITIES

17. Listen to the following recording of some African music. Observe how it uses different rhythms to create a polyrhythm.

4 Auditorium: Rock

A. The Facts

When **Elvis Presley** and **Chuck Berry** played their first songs, they probably did not imagine they were beginning a new era in the world of music. It was the 1950s and after that the guitar was the star of rock and roll music, just as the saxophone was for jazz.

In the 1970s came the British invasion of **The Beatles** and **The Rolling Stones** (seen as the good boys and the bad boys, respectively). They gave the final push to change rock and roll into rock music, with harder sounds and more provocative ideas.

A key guitarist in rock music was **Jimi Hendrix.** We consider him the father of 'distortion' (a powerful, harsh sound on the electric guitar). In the second half of the 20th century, terms like heavy metal, hard rock and grunge described music with a hard sound and a message of non-conformity.

B. The Music

A rock group typically has two electric guitars, one electric bass guitar, drums and a singer. This formation has changed over the years and sometimes includes instruments like the electric violin. We will listen to some representative sounds of rock.

Are you satisfied? Perhaps just the opposite. *(I Can't Get No) Satisfaction* by **The Rolling Stones** became a popular anthem for protest at the end of the 1960s.

Smoke on the Water by **Deep Purple** (Figure 2.6) starts with the most famous guitar *riff* of all time. The well-known introductory sequence consists of four riffs (phrases) with four measures. They each come in the following order:

1. Riff on the guitar
2. Riff on two guitars + drums (hi-hat)
3. Riff on two guitars + drums (hi-hat + snare)
4. Riff on two guitars + drums + bass guitar

The group **Iron Maiden** (Figure 2.7) had a solid, strong sound called heavy metal. The song *The Trooper* is a good example of their sound.

Who can recognise the powerful drums and the claps accompanying one of the most charismatic voices of rock? We are, of course, talking about Queen and the mythic song *We Will Rock You.*

Figure 2.6.
Concert with the legendary rock group **Deep Purple.**

Figure 2.7.
Image of the group **Iron Maiden** in concert. One of the founding fathers of heavy metal.

5 A Lot of Rhythm

In this lesson you will work with:

WORKSHEET

14. See the glossary: useful expressions in regard to rhythm.

Exercise 1. Do the following rhythmic exercises by clapping. Then try to play them one after the other with the recording playing in the background.

Exercise 2. Practise these polyrhythms by tapping both hands on your knees. You can also do them using bongos.

R. H.: small bongo
L. H.: large bongo

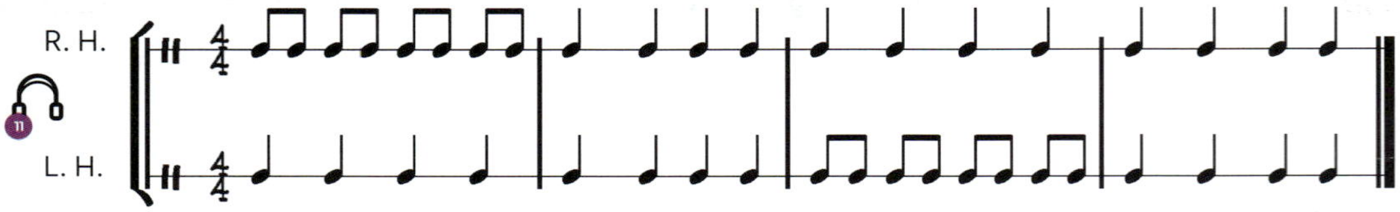

Exercise 3. Discover the drum kit (Figure 2.8):

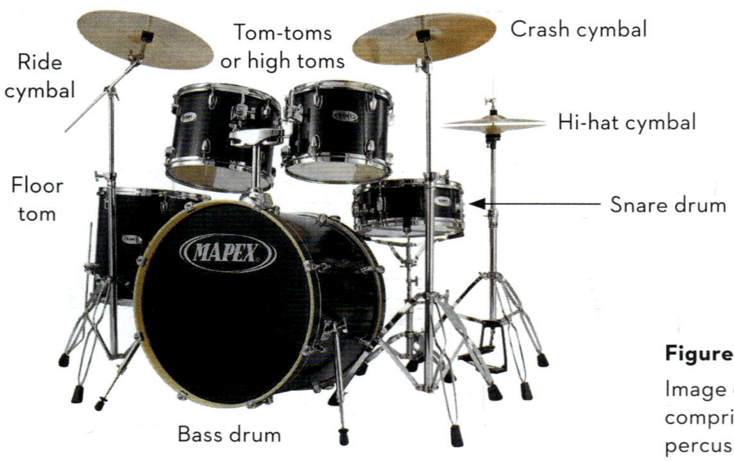

Figure 2.8. Image of a **drum kit** comprising different percussion instruments.

RESOURCES WEB

You can practise playing a virtual drum kit on the resources website.

6 In Tune

A. Train Your Voice

One of the main problems with singing is how high or low your voice can reach. In Unit 4 you will see that this range is called **tessitura.** It is normally more difficult to reach the high notes and people tend to 'scream' these notes. This makes them sound terrible and can also injure their vocal chords. Can you sing the high notes in your favourite songs?

The exercise in this unit will help you to increase the range of your voice to reach the highest notes. You can practise using the piano base in the resources for this unit.

Rising by semitones

WORKSHEET

15. If you want to train your voice and sing better with your friends, remember the page useful expressions in regard to singing.

B. Reading Music

In this unit we will work on reading and singing the notes we learned in Unit 1 – C, D and E – and we will add two new notes: F and G. Read the name of these notes to a beat. Try not to lose the beat as you read.

C. Performance Exercise

Now sing the following exercise. Sing the name of the notes, but try to pitch your voice well and do not sing from your throat. You can play the exercise on the recorder first to learn the correct pitch.

7 Move Your Fingers

WORKSHEET

16. See the glossary: useful expressions in regard to playing the recorder.

In this section we are going to look at a series of exercises to practise the low C and D. We will also continue to practise the notes from the previous unit: E, F, G, A and B.

Observe and memorise the finger positions for these notes in the Appendix. Then play the notes on your recorder. Take care to cover the holes completely and check each note sounds right.

Next, play the following exercises with the help of your teacher. Remember that you can use the accompaniments in the resources for this unit to help you practise at home or in the classroom.

Exercise 1 C-D-E

Exercise 2

Exercise 3 C-D-E-F-G

Exercise 4 C-D-E-F-G-A-B

Exercise 5

Exercise 6

Figure 2.9.
The **djembe** is an instrument from Africa. You can hear it on the accompaniment to Exercise 1.

Figure 2.10. A synthesiser.

8 Concert

One of the most internationally famous and veteran groups is **The Rolling Stones** (Figure 2.11). Their story began in 1961, when **Mick Jagger** and **Keith Richards** started to share their passion for music, especially for rhythm and blues.

Offstage the marketing experts wanted to brand them as the 'bad boys' of pop rock. This contrasted them with **The Beatles,** considered to be the 'good boys'.

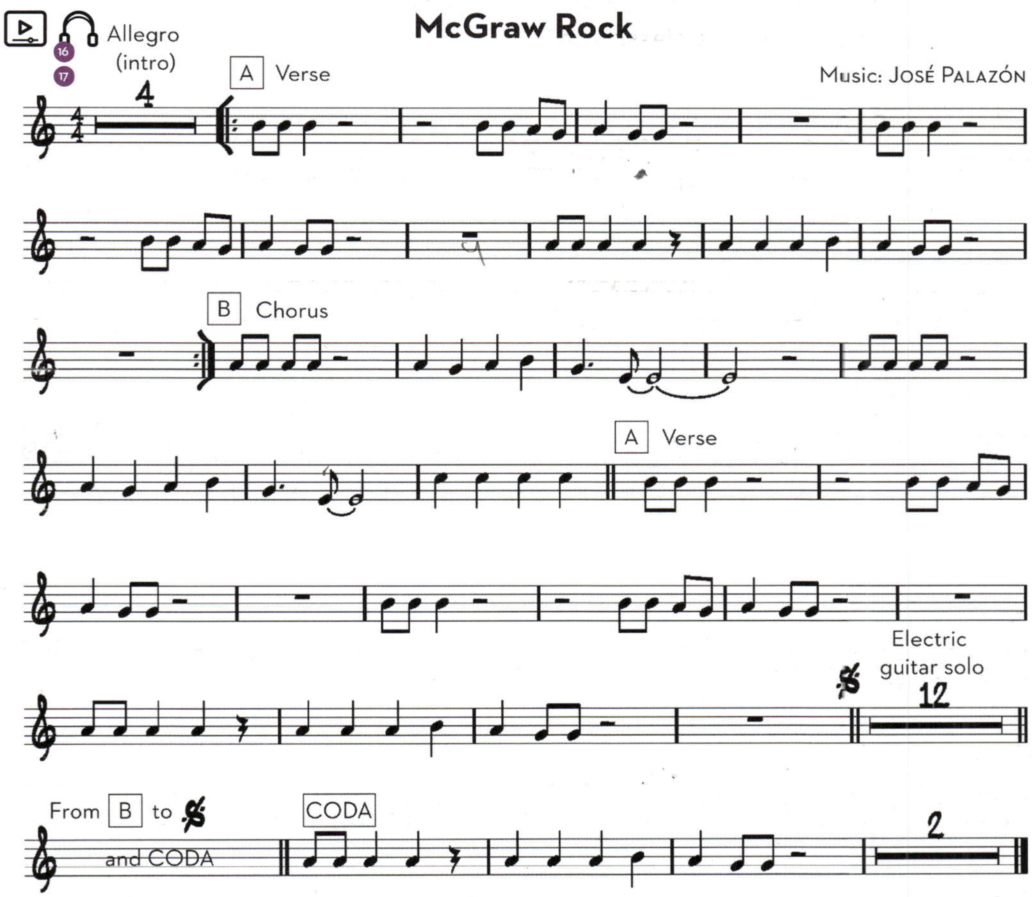

Figure 2.11.
The Rolling Stones in concert.

DID YOU KNOW?

Ties are signs used to add the duration of the notes together. We use ties if the notes have the same pitch or name.

This example shows a crotchet tied to a minim. You play the crotchet as if its value were three times as long as normal.

Rock and roll is a music genre with a marked rhythm and it is easy to dance to. It began in the 1950s and its influences include rhythm and blues and country music. Masters of the genre include Elvis Presley (also known as the King of Rock 'n' Roll), Chuck Berry and Little Richard. You are going to play a composition based on rock and roll from the 1950s, but with diverse musical influences.

Figure 2.12.
Elvis Presley.

Rock and Sol

REMEMBER

Repetition Signs

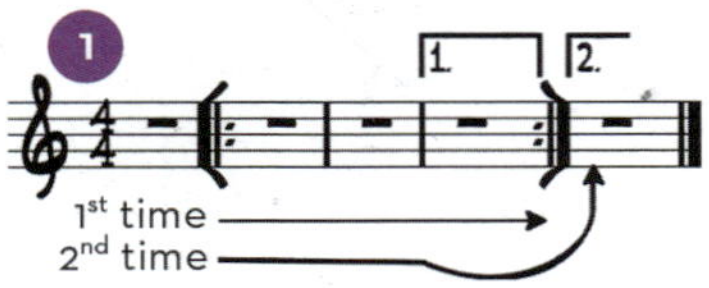

1st and 2nd bracket. When we play the 2nd repetition, we skip the 1st bracket and play the 2nd bracket instead.

Repeat the two bars immediately before.

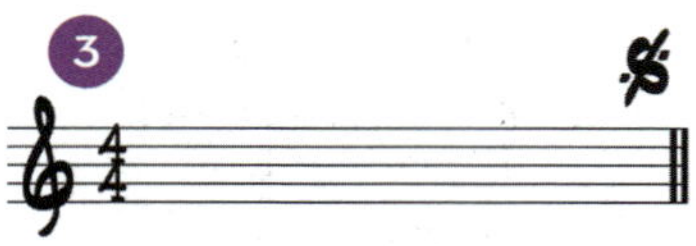

This sign indicates a jump from the place it appears to another part of the sheet music.

Download and print the worksheet you will find in the OLC to complete the concept map of the unit.

B... → **T...** →

- *Presto* (V... f...)
- *Allegro* (F...)
- *Andante* (Me...)
- *Adagio* (Sl...)
- *Largo* (V... sl...)
- *Accelerando* (In... fas...)
- *Ritardando* (In... sl...)

T...: Sp... of the beat

Measured with me...

B...: I... pu... of the music

Accent → **Me...**

- Ac... e... two beats → Du... meter
- Ac... every three beats → Tr... meter
- Ac... every four beats → Qu... meter

Rhythm — The co... of sounds of different du... that fl... around a b... .

Polyrh... — The s... of different rh... .

Remember

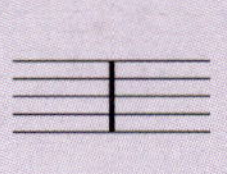

We use the **bar line** used to se... the measures.

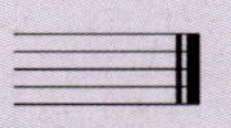

The **bold double** bar line is at the end of the sheet music. It tells us where a piece of music fi... .

The **tie** un... two notes of the same n... or p... . It lasts for the sum of their du... .

1st and 2nd brackets. When playing the 2nd repetition, we skip the 1st bracket and play the 2... bracket instead.

FINAL ACTIVITIES

1. Define the concepts of *beat* and *tempo*.
2. In your Workbook write each of the following indications and their meaning in the correct column: *allegro, forte, adagio, piano, presto, fortissimo, largo, pianissimo, crescendo, accelerando, ritardando, diminuendo, andante y mezzoforte*.

Tempo	Dynamics
Allegro (fast)	*Forte* (loud)
accelerando	forte
ritardando	piano
presto	fortissimo
adagio	pianissimo
largo	crescendo
andante	diminuendo
allegro	mezzoforte

3. Next to each diagram, write the type of meter it represents:

> >
| | | |
1 2 1 2 — duple meter

> >
| | | | | |
1 2 3 1 2 3 — triple meter

> >
| | | | | | | |
1 2 3 4 1 2 3 4 — quadruple meter

4. Put the bar lines in the correct place:

5. **Complete the following measures with the correct note values or rests:**

6. **Some measures contain errors. Find them.**

7. **Rhythmic dictation: listen to the rhythmic schemes your teacher plays and write them in your Workbook.**

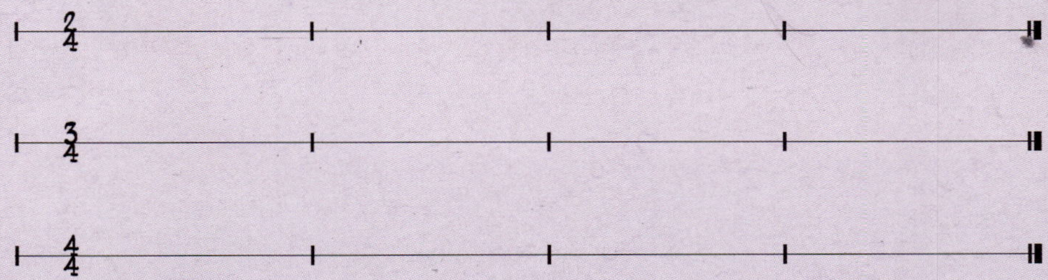

Listening x

FINAL PROJECT

In groups of 4 or 5

1. You have made rhythm with: ... (Think of objects in your class).
2. You will create a polyrhythm with those objects, with instruments in the classroom or instruments you have got at home and you can bring to class.
3. Repeat to do a good performance.
4. Show the polyrhythms to the rest of the class.
5. Listen to your classmates' rhythms and give them marks.
6. You will perform the best polyrhythm together.
7. Now you have a good rhythmic base. You can create an English rap to sing over it.
8. Who is the best rap group?

3 MELODY AND HARMONY

The ***melody*** is the part of music that we perceive most easily and the easiest part for us to remember.

It can change our mood and make us happy, sad, excited and so on. As a result, the final sound of the music depends on the type of melody it has.

Meanwhile, the ***harmony*** gives the accompaniment that complements and enriches the melody and helps to define its character.

In this unit we will explain some of the characteristics we use to analyse a melody and you will learn more about the concept of harmony.

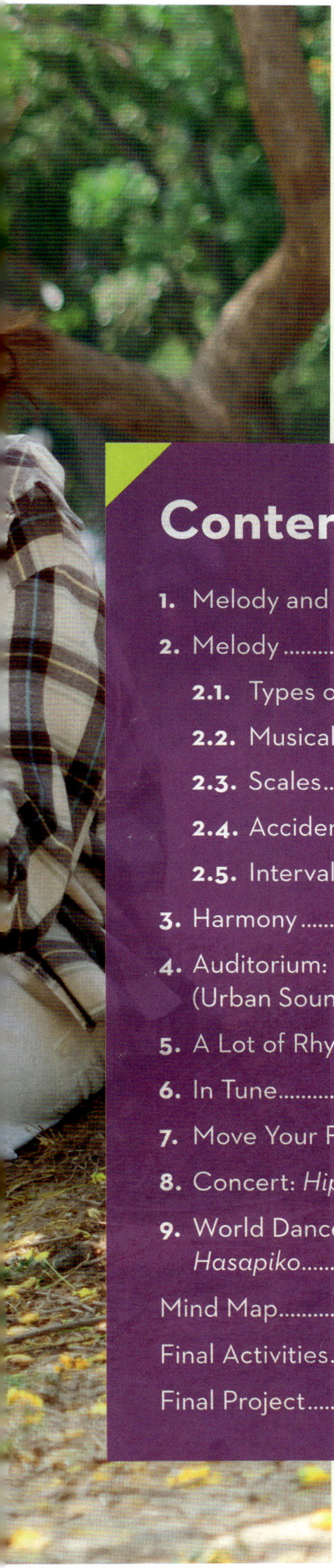

Contents

WORK ON THE TEXT

Read with your teacher, download the worksheet and fill in the gaps.

1. The m ... is the part of music that we p ... most easily and the easiest part to r ... .
2. It can ch ... our m ... and make us happy, sad, excited and so on.
3. Meanwhile the harmony gives the a ... that complements and e ... the melody.
4. In this unit we will learn to a ... se a melody and more about h ... .

WARM UP

1. Think on melodies you know or you like. Could you give an adjective or mood for every melody?
2. Think of instruments that can accompany melodies by playing the harmony and chords (harmonic instruments). Make a list. You will share it afterwards with your partner.
3. You can find apps on the internet to compose and analyse music.

FIND A CLASSMATE

In pairs or groups of 4.

1. Can you hum a melody to your partner? Share your melodies and make a list with all the famous melodies you remember with their moods. Do you know the names of those songs? (chart in the OLC)
2. Share your list of harmonic instruments with your classmate.

KEYWORDS

Download and print the activities that will guide you through the essential vocabulary of this unit.

1 Melody and Harmony

WORKSHEET

1. Download and complete to understand better.
   a) 'Successive' means: one ... .
   b) 'Simultaneous' means: at the ... .
2. Assign the 6 sentences to the right element of music: Harmony or Melody. See the diagram in the OLC.

Imagine you want to tell a friend about the latest song by your favourite singer. When you hum the song for them, the part you hum is the *melody*. However, the song probably has other instruments (keyboard, guitar, bass) accompanying the main melody. These give the *harmony*. Finally, the drums give the music a rhythmic base.

If we combine sounds with different pitches one after another, we can create a **melody.** If we also play different sounds at the same time, we have the **harmony.**

Melody: successive sounds **Harmony:** simultaneous sounds

ACTIVITIES

1. **Listen to the following recording called *Fiesta pagana* by the group Mägo de Oz (Figure 3.1):**
   a) Identify the melody. Which instruments are participating?
   b) Which instrument plays the harmonic accompaniment?

Figure 3.1.
Mägo de Oz. Spanish rock group.

The melody is represented *horizontally:* the sounds are next to each other. But, the harmony is represented *vertically:* the sounds are on top of each other to show they play at the same time.

ACTIVITIES

2. **Listen to the following three fragments. In your Workbook match them to the correct option: melody / harmony / melody and harmony. Write these words in the order in which you hear them.**

2 Melody

As we just learned, **melody** is a succession of sounds with different pitches. The sounds are driven by the rhythm and express a musical idea.

The same succession of sounds (or pitches) can sound very different depending on the rhythm. Try it with the activity below.

ACTIVITIES

3. Listen to the melody your teacher is going to play. It is very well known, but we have modified the rhythm so it is almost impossible to recognise. Can you identify it?

Copy just the heads of the notes into your Workbook. If you still do not recognise the piece, try playing it on the recorder. Play all the notes as if they were crotchets. Do you know which melody it is now?

WORKSHEET

3. Choose the correct words in the right order to make the definition of MELODY.
   a) Of different pitches
   b) To express a musical idea
   c) Simultaneous sounds
   d) One after the other
   e) Succesive sounds
   f) At the same time
   g) Successive rhythms
   h) Sounds are driven by the rhythm
4. Do the other activities about melody in the OLC.

In the following sections, you will learn some of the characteristics that determine the character of a melody.

WORKSHEET

5. Download and match the drawing with the right word in the OLC charts.
6. Draw and write the melodic profile in the OLC charts.

2.1. Types of Melodies

There are many types of melodies depending on their design or **melodic profile:**

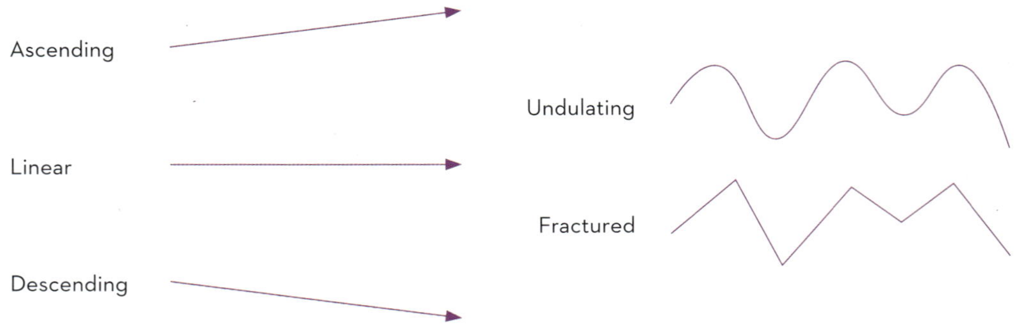

ACTIVITIES

4. Observe the following melodies. Imagine a line connecting the heads of all the notes in each example. Which type of melodic profile appears? Draw each profile in your Workbook.

Melody 1. Introduction to *Symphony Nº 1* by **Beethoven.**

Melody 2. *The Good, the Bad and the Ugly* by **Ennio Morricone.**

Melody 3. *The Lord of the Rings* (Figure 3.2) by **H. Shore.**

Melody 4. *Samba de uma nota só* by **Jobim.**

Melody 5. *Adagio* by **Albinoni.**

5. Now listen to the pieces and identify the order in which they are played.

Figure 3.2.
Image from **The Lord of the Rings, Tolkien**'s trilogy adapted for the big screen.

2.2. Musical Phrases

Melodies use **musical phrases** in their structure, divided like written or spoken language. Just as a paragraph has different sentences, we can also separate a melody into several musical phrases.

Musical phrases are usually separated by *cadences* or pauses. These are the equivalent to the punctuation marks in written language. These cadences can be:

- ***Imperfect:*** leaving the musical idea in suspense, giving the feeling of something unfinished **(,)**.
- ***Perfect:*** giving a sense of finality, of relaxation, of the musical idea coming to an end **(.)**.

ACTIVITIES

6. Are the following musical phrases imperfect (I) or perfect (P):

1 ... 2 ... 3 ... 4 ... 5 ... 6 ...

The phrases you just heard form part of three melodies. Match each imperfect cadence to its corresponding perfect cadence. Do you know any of the melodies?

1 and ... ... and ... ... and ...

2.3. Scales

We construct the melody inside a specific organisation of pitches of sound called a *scale*.

A **scale** is a succession of sounds ordered from low to high, or vice versa. It is the set of sounds a composer will use to create his/her work.

ACTIVITIES

7. Look at the following melody:

Find the correct stave (or staff in the USA) in your Workbook. Now write the different notes that appear in the melody, but do not repeat any of them and put them in order from low to high.

When all the notes from the melody are on the stave, can you say which scale it is?

WORKSHEET

7. Put the keywords in the right place to define imperfect and perfect cadences:

   Suspense / finality / coming to an end / unfinished / perfect cadence / imperfect cadence.

8. Choose the correct words in the right order to make the definition of SCALE:

   To create a work / chosen by a composer / succesion of sounds / ordered from low to high.

9. Do the other fun activities in the OLC.

REMEMBER

Additional lines or ledger lines (USA): these are extra lines placed above or below the stave. We use them to write higher or lower notes that do not fit on the normal five-line stave.

Example:

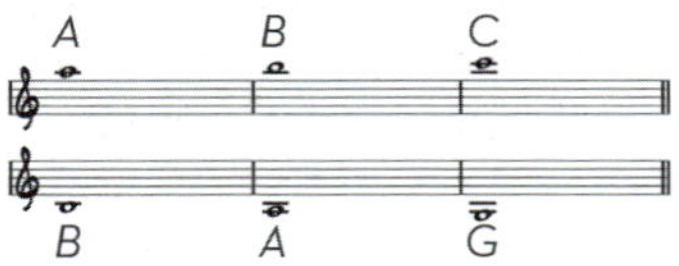

WORKSHEET

10. Draw and translate.

    Copy the drawing of the scale in OLC activities and translate the titles.

    Do the same with the other scales. Compare them.

11. Do the accidentals matching cards activity.
12. Do the other fun activities in the OLC.

CURIOUS FACTS

In oriental music, they often use the pentatonic scale. It only has five notes and gives music a particular sound we associate with an exotic quality.

The difference between two consecutive notes in a scale can be a *tone* or a *semitone* (half a tone). The distribution of these tones and semitones can be different. This means we can distinguish between major and minor scales. The major scales use the *C major* scale as a model. The minor scales use the *A minor* scale as a model. The scale we choose contributes to the character of the piece.

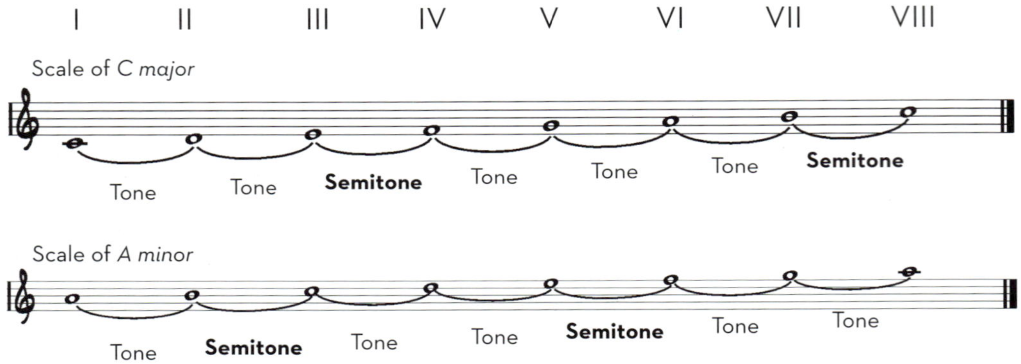

Notice that the semitones are always between the notes *E-F* and *B-C*, but they are in different places in the scales. This is why each scale gives music a different character. Each note of a scale has a special name, called a scale degree. The first and last note is called the tonic. The fifth note is called the dominant.

ACTIVITIES

5 **8. Listen to the following two recordings. They have the same melody but one is in major and the other in minor. Can you tell the difference? Which one uses a major scale and which one uses a minor scale?**

2.4. Accidentals

Not all scales use natural sounds. Some scales use altered sounds or accidentals.

Accidentals are signs used to modify the pitch of the sound. We write them to the left of the note, at the same height as the note head.

- **Sharp** ♯ Raises the pitch a semitone
- **Flat** ♭ Lowers the pitch a semitone
- **Natural** ♮ Cancels the effect of the sharp and the flat

2.5. Intervals

Just as we calculate the distance between two points, we can measure the distance between the pitch of one note and another.

The distance in pitch between two notes is an **interval.**

To name an interval, count from the first to the last note, both included. The resulting interval takes an ordinal number.

Example:

Between C and A there are six notes, so we say there is a sixth interval between them.

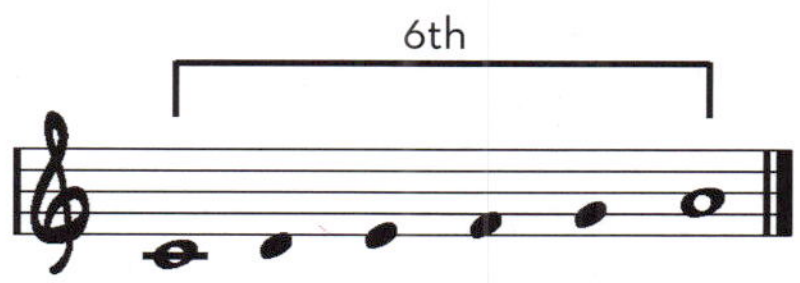

Observe the intervals between C and the rest of the notes in the scale. You will notice that the 8th interval is the same note in a different pitch.

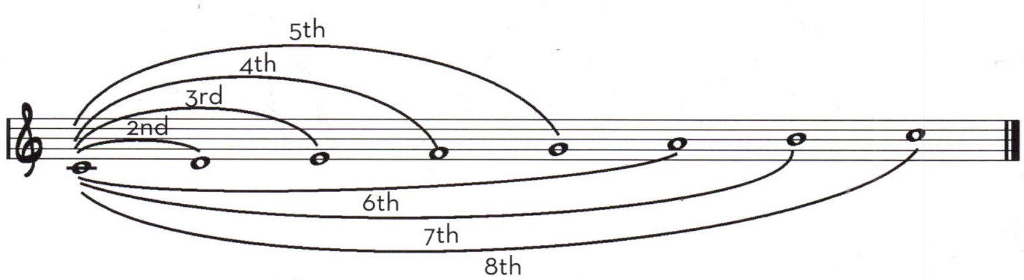

Intervals can be *ascending* (rising from low to high) or *descending* (falling from high to low). We can also classify intervals as *melodic* or *harmonic*. In melodic intervals, the two notes in the interval play one after another. In harmonic intervals, these notes sound at the same time.

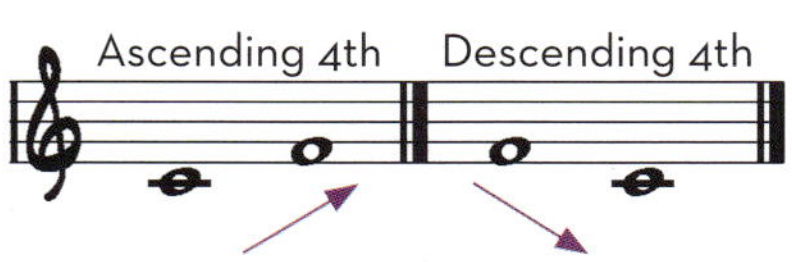

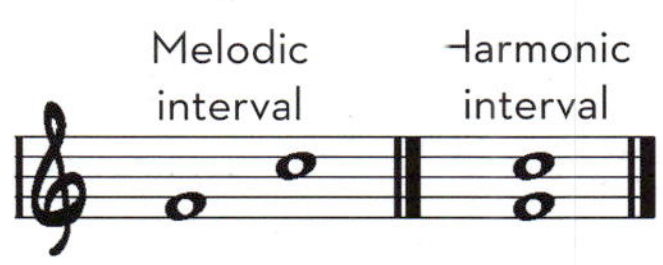

ACTIVITIES

9. **Copy these intervals into your Workbook and name them:**

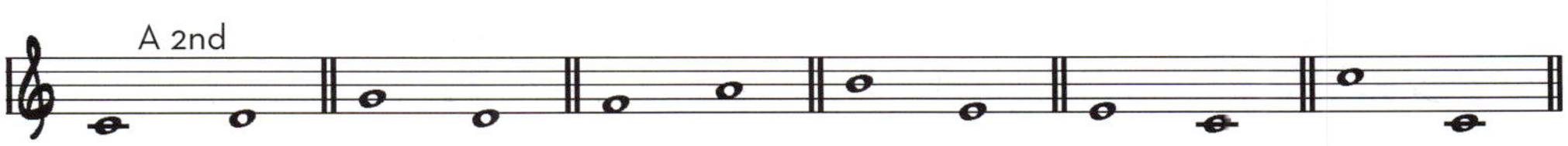

10. **Listen to the intervals your teacher will play. Say if they are ascending or descending.**

DID YOU KNOW?

In the solar system, all the planets orbit the Sun. Something similar happens with musical scales: the most important note is C. It is called the tonic and all the other notes 'gravitate' around it.

WORKSHEET

13. Can you say what an interval is?

    Do you count the distance like in maths?

14. Download and do the other activities about intervals in the OLC.

3 Harmony

The term **harmony** is related to the organisation of simultaneous sounds. The harmony accompanies the melody and enriches it, helping to define its character. The same melody can sound very different if we change the harmonic accompaniment.

ACTIVITIES

11. Listen to this recording. First, you will hear a melody. Then you will hear the same melody with two different accompaniments. Notice how the harmony enriches the melody and gives it a more musical character.

When we combine various different sounds at the same time, we can produce two different feelings in the listener:

- Feeling of relaxation: in music we call this **consonance.**
- Feeling of tension: we call this **dissonance.**

Alternating between these two feelings (tension and relaxation) is the basis for musical creation.

ACTIVITIES

12. Listen to the previous recording again. Which of the two harmonic accompaniments do you think is more consonant and which is more dissonant? Give reasons for your answer.

The basis for harmony is the **chord**. A chord is the combination of two or three different sounds that we hear at the same time.

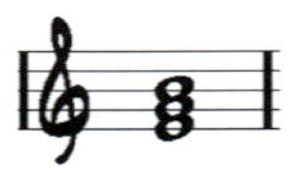

The most usual way of creating chords in music is overlapping third intervals with a specific note.

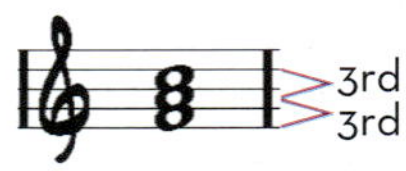

ACTIVITIES

13. In your Workbook build chords around the following notes:

WORKSHEET

15. Download and answer the questions:
   a) What is the function of harmony?
   b) With harmony we can produce c ... or d ... .
   c) What is the difference?
   d) How many sounds do we need to make a chord?
   e) How do we create chords with a specific note?

4 Auditorium: Hip-Hop / Rap (Urban Sounds)

WORKSHEET

16. Listen to the excerpts and make your ideal list of hip-hop musical hits by filling in the listening chart (OLC).
17. Read or listen to your teacher and complete the 'Five W' activity, glossary and listening chart about this page.

A. The Facts

The rivalry or tension between artists has always been a constant in all types of art: **Leonardo da Vinci/Michelangelo** in painting; **Brahms/Wagner** in classical music; and **Bird/Coltrane** in jazz.

A style of music created in the African-American and Hispanic neighbourhoods of New York embraced this competitive spirit more than any other. The people from these areas played with words, mockery and insults. This art led to a musical culture known as **hip-hop** and a verbal battle began between the 'MCs' and the 'rappers' (Figure 3.3).

The term 'rap' meant 'talk' in the jargon of the 1970s. Rap refers to the music, but hip-hop refers more widely to the music, the new graffiti culture, the style of dressing and above all the breakdancing.

Figure 3.3.
Image of a performance by rappers.

B. The Music 7

One of the most recognisable sound effects in hip-hop is 'scratching'. The first DJs (disc jockeys) used this technique. It consists of moving a vinyl record backwards and forwards with your fingers to repeat a sound.

Listen to **DJ Qbert** on the track *Electric Scratch Dome*. We consider him one of the best scratch DJs in the world.

Disco and funk from the 1970s influenced rap music. Rap inherited the simple and danceable drum designs from disco. From funk came the complex bass lines and highly rhythmic guitar riffs. Listen to *Rapper's Delight* (1979) by **Sugar Hills** and identify the elements we mention.

We close this auditorium with the track *Gangsta's Paradise* by **Coolio.** The song is based on the melody *Pastime Paradise* by **Stevie Wonder.** It appeared on the soundtrack for the film *Dangerous Minds* and reached number 1 in the American charts. It also reached number 1 in the United Kingdom and was the first rap single to sell a million copies there.

Songs by **Public Enemy, Eminem, L.L. Cool J, Beastie Boys. Ice-T, Ice Cube, 50 Cent,** etc. still have lots of violence in their content. The Spanish music scene includes rap artists such as **SFDK, El club de los poetas violentos, El Chojin, Violadores del verso, Nach** and so on. In Brazil they use hip-hop as a medium for social inclusion. **Nega Gizza,** one of the best-known rappers in Brazil, uses the music to denounce politics. He sings about issues such as violence, drugs, prostitution and poverty.

Beginning of the lyrics to the song *Rapper's Delight:*

I said a hip hop the hippie the hippie to the hip hip hop, a you don't stop

The rock it to the bang bang boogie say up jumped the boogie

To the rhythm of the boogie, the beat

You can also search for the original video of this song on YouTube.

WORKSHEET

18. If you want to train your voice and sing with your friends better, see the final glossary: useful expressions in regard to rhythm in the OLC.

5 A Lot of Rhythm

We are going to look more at the note values and rests we saw in the previous unit and practise other new ones.

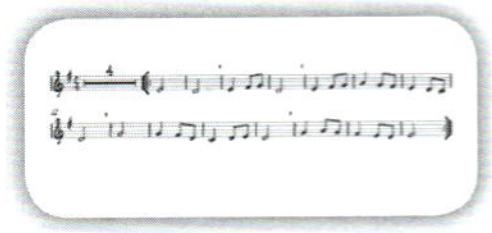

Do the following rhythmic exercises by clapping. Then play them one after the other with the background recording:

Exercise 1

Exercise 2

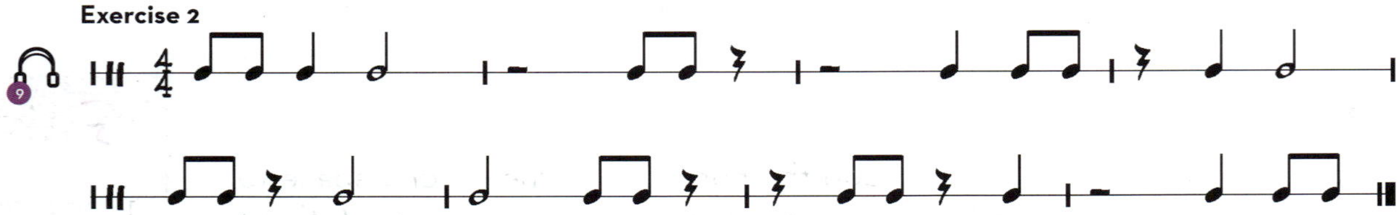

Practise these polyrhythms by tapping both hands on your knees. You can also do them using bongos:

Exercise 3

Exercise 4

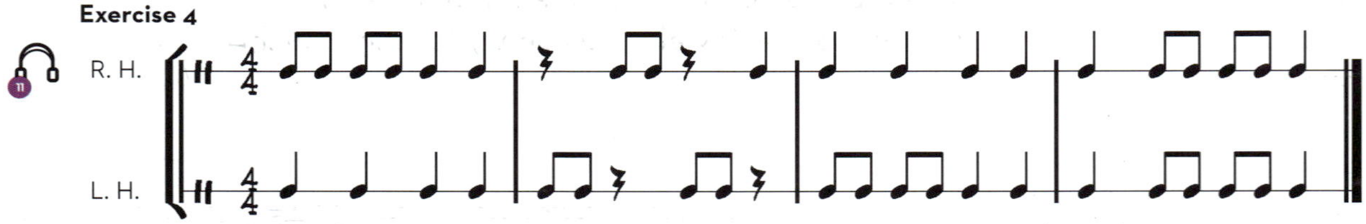

Let us learn a little more about the drums. In the musical example below, you can see how some of the instruments in a drum kit are represented in graphic form. Listen to the three instruments on the recording in the resources for this unit.

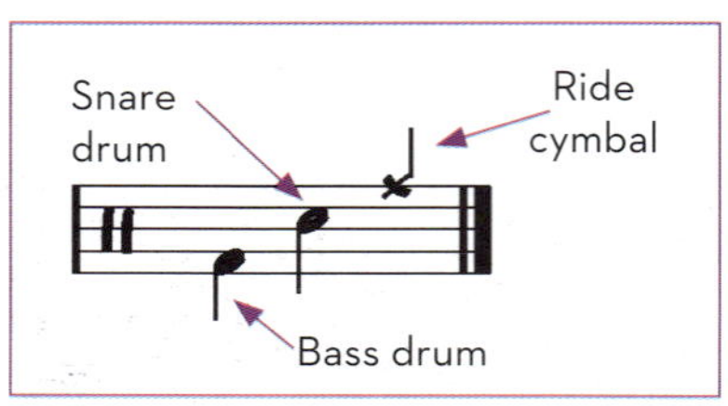

6 In Tune

A. Train Your Voice

As you know, jumping over an obstacle can sometimes be dangerous because we can trip over it. Well, vocal jumps from a lower note to a higher one or vice versa can also be problematic for singers with little experience. With these jumps or melodic intervals, at first it is normal to sing out of tune on the higher note. This exercise will help you improve your tuning in the 3rd and 5th intervals.

DID YOU KNOW?

Lots of people speak in a lower tone than their natural one. This can cause problems, including losing their voice and injuring their vocal chords.

B. Reading Music

On this occasion we are going to add the note *A* from the second space to those you already know. Mark a beat of approximately crotchet = 80. Without breaking the beat, say the name of these notes (without singing).

WORKSHEET

19. See the glossary: useful expressions in regard to singing.

C. Repertoire

With the notes and exercises you have studied so far, you are now ready to play a song. Let's start with a piece of music from an aboriginal tribe in Australia. It is a canon, so when you know it well, you can try to sing it in the round.

Interpretive Suggestion

UNISON	MELODY AND *OSTINATO*	CANON WITH TWO VOICES
	– 2nd voice sings *ostinato* in C (same lyrics).	– Start with a difference of four bars. – End when 2nd voice completes the melody.

WORKSHEET

20. See final glossary: useful expressions in regard to playing the recorder.

Figure 3.4.
A group of jazz musicians.

7 Move Your Fingers

Continuing with the recorder course, in this unit we are going to revise the notes we studied earlier. We will also learn to play *quavers* with our instrument. Follow your teacher's instructions and remember the advice from the previous units (especially on the regular emission of sound) to obtain a pleasant sound.

As usual, we can use two different accompaniments included in the resources for this unit:

- Accompaniment for Exercises 1, 2 and 3: *drums, electric bass, synthesisers* and the *gaita*, a typical instrument from Galician folklore.
- Accompaniment for Exercises 4, 5 and 6: a jazz trio (Figure 3.4) with a *piano, drums* and *double bass*.

Exercise 1

Exercise 2

Exercise 3

Exercise 4

Exercise 5

Exercise 6

8 Concert

In the *Auditorium* section of this unit, you have detailed information about hip-hop. Did you notice the simplicity of the music? What about the use of simple, repetitive rhythms on the drums?

These techniques mean you can understand the lyrics better. As you know, the most important thing in rap is the story it tells. Rappers do not say, 'I'm going to sing,' they say, 'I'm going to rhyme.' Did you notice that their lyrics rhyme a lot? The rhyme is more important than melody in rap. In fact, most of the rhyming phrases do not have a melody, but a very precise rhythm. The piece you are going to perform has some musical elements used in rap: a strong rhythmic base, scratch effects and simple melodic designs. But it has a more elaborate melody and harmony. This is because it is an instrumental piece and does not depend on lyrics.

Figure 3.5.

A rap group performing on stage.

Hip-Night-Hop

17 18 Recorder

Music: José Palazón

WORKSHEET

21. Download and answer.

Do you remember what the characteristics of Hip Hop music are?

1. S ... .
2. Use of s ... and r ... rhythms on the d ... .
3. The most important thing is the s ... .
4. Rappers don't sing but r ... .
5. Sometimes there are s ... effects.
6. And simple m ... designs.

9 World Dance Workshop

In this workshop we are going to discover more about some traditional dances from around the world. The best way to learn them is by dancing!

In this unit we will learn a **Greek dance.** Greece has an extraordinary wealth of music and traditional dances. They are still very present in everyday Greek life and are also popular abroad. This is helped by films such as *Zorba the Greek*.

Greek dances are very similar to one another. They usually involve placing your hands firmly on the shoulders of the people next to you. The dancers are often in the same formation. The circle is a fundamental shape, whether closed or open. The linked arms or the arms around the shoulders form a chain. The leader of an open circle adds to the dance steps, giving them extra colour. This transforms a simple repetition of steps into an exciting performance. When someone stands up to dance in Greece, it does not matter what their social background or financial situation is: 'They are king while they dance.'

The dance we are going to perform is called ***Hasapiko.*** It is one of the most traditional dances in Greece. The formation can be a line or a circle with your hands on the shoulders of the people standing next to you. In many choreographies the dance begins slowly and gradually becomes faster. It often includes jumps. You are not going to start slowly or jump in this version. The melody to dance the Hasapiko is called *Oloi oi rempetes*, performed by the celebrated Greek singer and guitarist Giorgos Ntalaras.

DID YOU KNOW?

The famous *Sirtaki* is not a traditional Greek dance. It was created in 1964 for the film *Zorba the Greek*. It is a mixture of slow and fast versions of the *Hasapiko* dance.

WORKSHEET

22. Make your own glossary: useful expressions in regard to dancing with the most common expressions used to indicate instructions for dancing.

Choreography Summary

The dance you are going to perform starts with all the participants in a circle. At first the dancers hold the shoulders of the two people standing next to them. (Later on, your arms are in the shape of a W).

Your legs step from side to side, alternating between three, two and one step(s). This makes the circle close slightly. Finally, it returns to the initial position as the dancers take a few steps back.

Download and print the worksheet you will find in the OLC to complete the concept map of the unit.

- **Pitch**
  - **Melody** S ... of sounds
  - **Harmony** S ... sounds
- **M ...**
  - T ... of melodies: A ... D ... L ... U ... F ...
  - Musical p ... separated by C ...
    - I ...
    - Perfect (.)
  - S ...
    - S ... of sounds ordered from l ... to high; these can be
      - Major (h ...)
      - M ... (s ...)
    - Distribution of tones and semitones in a major scale
      - Scale of C major: Tone, Tone, S ..., Tone, Tone, Tone, S ...
  - A ...
    - **Sharp** ♯ R ... the pitch a semitone
    - **Flat** ♭ L ... the pitch a semitone
    - **Natural** ♮ C ... the effect of the sharp and the flat
  - I ...
    - A ... 4th, D ... 4th — Classification of the intervals according to the d ... of the notes
    - M ... interval, H ... interval — Classification of the intervals according to the o ... of sounds
- **H ...**
  - C ... of three or more sounds
    - C ... (relaxation)
    - D ... (tension)
  - is based on the C ...: Set of three or more different s ... which play at the same t ...

1. Answer the following questions:

a) In the following examples, identify which one shows a melody and which one shows a harmony. Explain your answer.

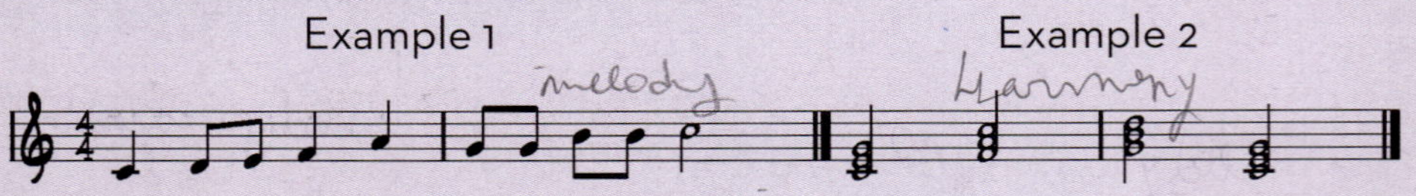

2. What is a *scale*? Draw the scale of C on a stave and indicate where the tones and semitones are.

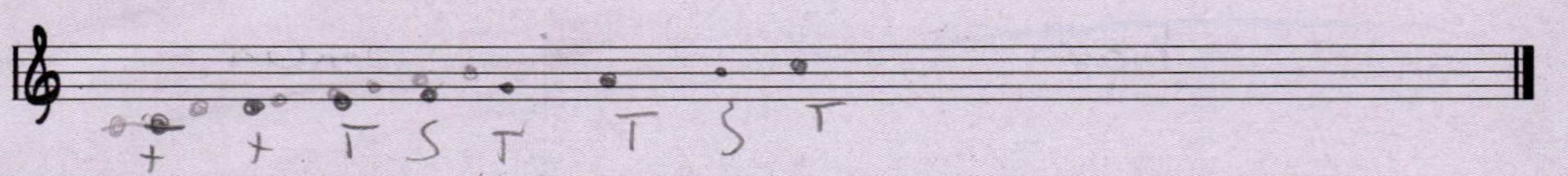

3. Do the following activities on accidentals in your Workbook.

- Sharp
- Flat
- Natural

a) Write a sharp for all the *F* notes and a flat for all the *D* notes. Remember that we write the accidentals to the left of the note, at the same height.

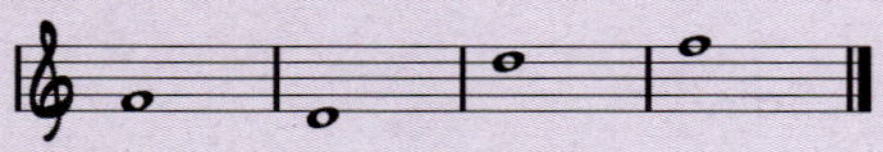

b) Identify the lowest sound in each of the following pairs.

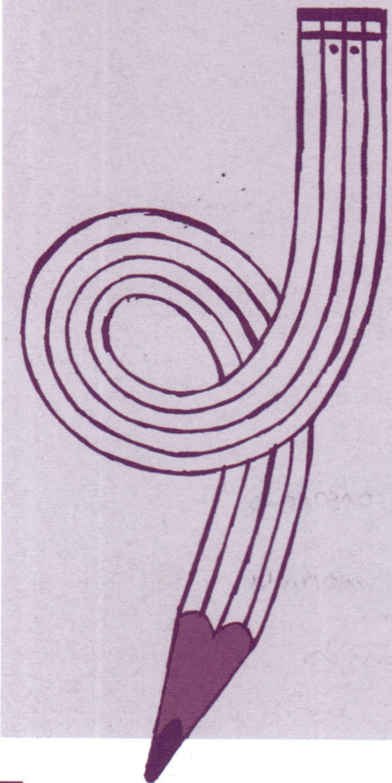

4. Answer the following questions on musical intervals.

a) What is an interval?

b) Write a melodic interval and a harmonic interval using *E*.

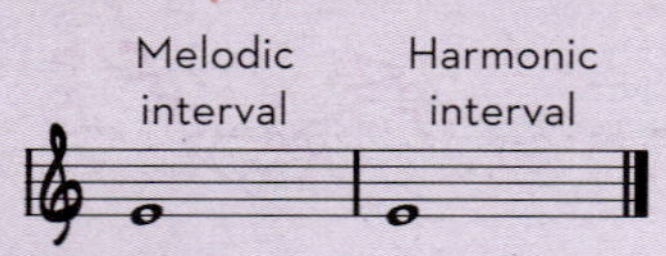

5. Name the following intervals:

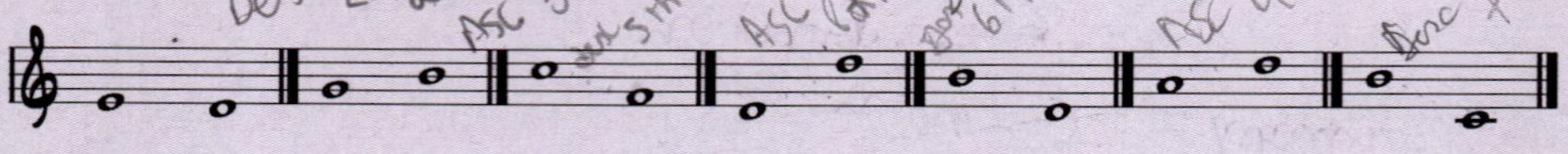

6. Complete the following intervals from the note given:

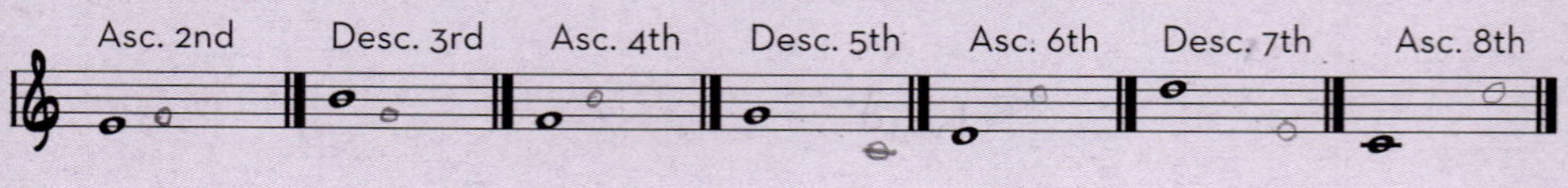

7. **Show what you know about musical chords.**

a) What is a *chord*?

b) Can you play a chord on your recorder? Why or why not? What about with a guitar?

c) Divide the class into three groups. Each group will play a note from the chord.

	Group 1	Group 2	Group 3
First chord			
Second chord			

- Which of the two chords creates a feeling of relaxation and which one a feeling of tension?
- Keeping this answer in mind, which is consonant and which is dissonant?

8. **Do you recognise these melodies?**

a) 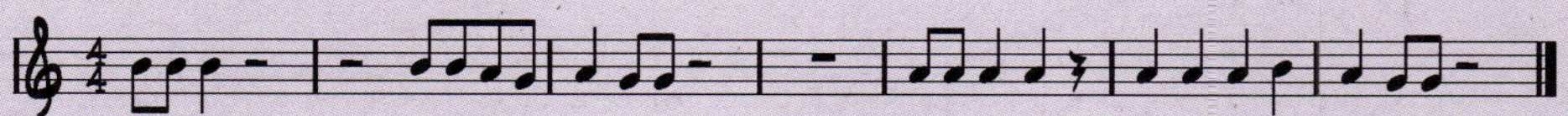

b) 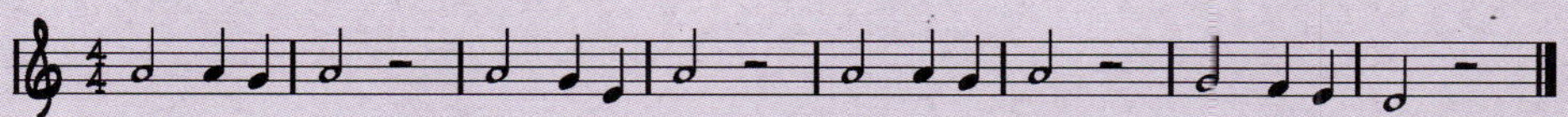

9. **A fragmented melody.**

Here is a series of disordered fragments from a melody that has appeared in this unit. Play each fragment with the recorder. Can you put the fragments into the correct order and identify the melody?

a) 

b) 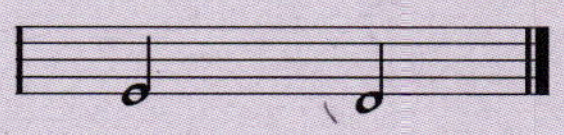

c) 

d) 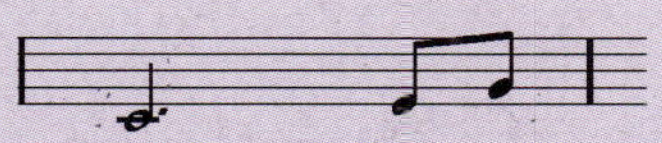

FINAL PROJECT

In groups of 4

1. Create a melody at home with 4 bars in the scale of C major for the recorder.
2. Share it with your group.
3. Choose the two or three best melodies.
4. Make a song combining the melodies. Change the cadences (suspensive or conclusive) to make a structured song.
5. Write the lyrics.
6. Perform the song for the class or record yourselves singing it.
7. Do a contest to choose the winner of the best song composer of the class.

4 VOICE

'Song is the human voice expressing itself with music. It is a marvellous and delicate instrument. We cannot see it because it is inside us. It is subject to our joys, emotions and sadness, to different physical states, to the changes in weather. In short, to everything that affects us in one way or another' (Isabela Marí).

Humans have used their **voice** as a means of expression and communication since ancient times. The voice is the oldest instrument in existence. In this unit you will learn how it works and its great musical possibilities.

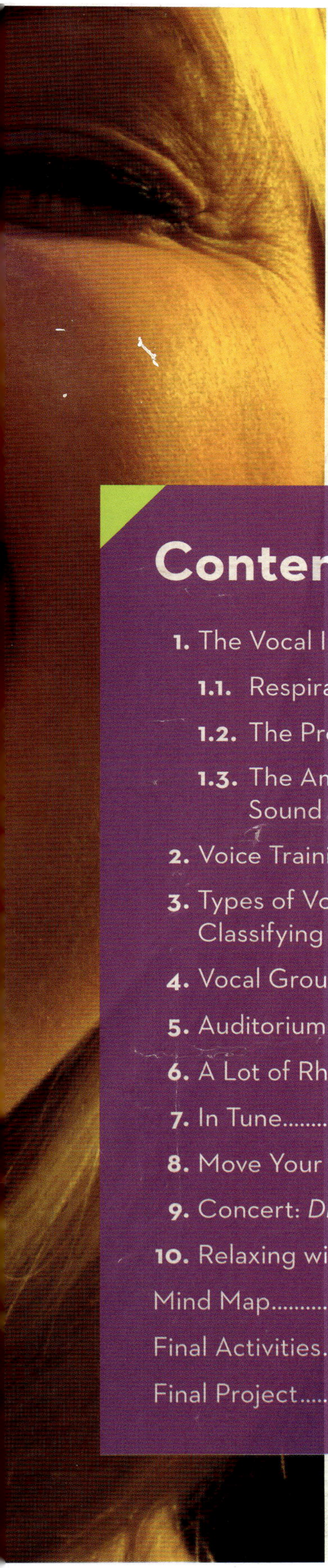

Contents

WORK ON THE TEXT

Don´t open your book.
Listen to your teacher, download and answer the questions.
What is the oldest instrument in existence?

WARM UP

Download, answer the questions and share your answers with your partner and teacher.

1. Search for *Voice Kids* on YouTube.
2. Search for *Les Choristes* on YouTube or watch the trailer of the film.
3. Search for a documentary on YouTube about children's choirs like *Angelic Voices: the Choristers of Salisbury Cathedral* or *A day in the life of a chorister at Canterbury Cathedral.*

FIND A CLASSMATE

1. Compare with your classmate and add more words to the glossary.
2. Finally we will complete the chart on the blackboard.
3. In the final activities we will choose the most important terms and make a concept map with them.

KEYWORDS

Individually, scan the pictures and graphics in the text (pages 62-69) in 1 minute and try to find the keywords that we will learn in the unit. Fill in the glossary in the OLC.

WORKSHEET

1. Download and make a diagram with the 3 processes involved in the vocal apparatus. Cut the parts out and order them. Ask your partner and swap your parts.
2. Download and make a jumbled word activity. Label Figure 4.1 about respiration in the OLC.

1 The Vocal Instrument

Have you ever stopped to think that we all have a musical instrument in our bodies? It is also the oldest instrument in the world. We are talking about the voice.

A violinist must know exactly how their violin works to play music on it. In the same way, it is important to understand how our voice works to sing and even talk properly.

We call the parts of our body responsible for digesting food the digestive system. Similarly, we call the parts of our body that produce our voice the **vocal apparatus.**

There are three processes involved: respiration, the production of sound and the amplification of this sound in the resonators.

1.1. Respiration

For the voice to make sound, there must be an adequate flow of air when we breathe: during inhalation and during exhalation.

Between the **lungs** and the digestive system there is a muscle called the **diaphragm** (Figure 4.1). It plays a very important role in singing because it helps to push the air out when we exhale.

The effect is similar to pressing a rubber ring to deflate it: the air is expelled with much more force. Also, we can make the air come out steadily even when there is only a little left inside. Look at this diagram:

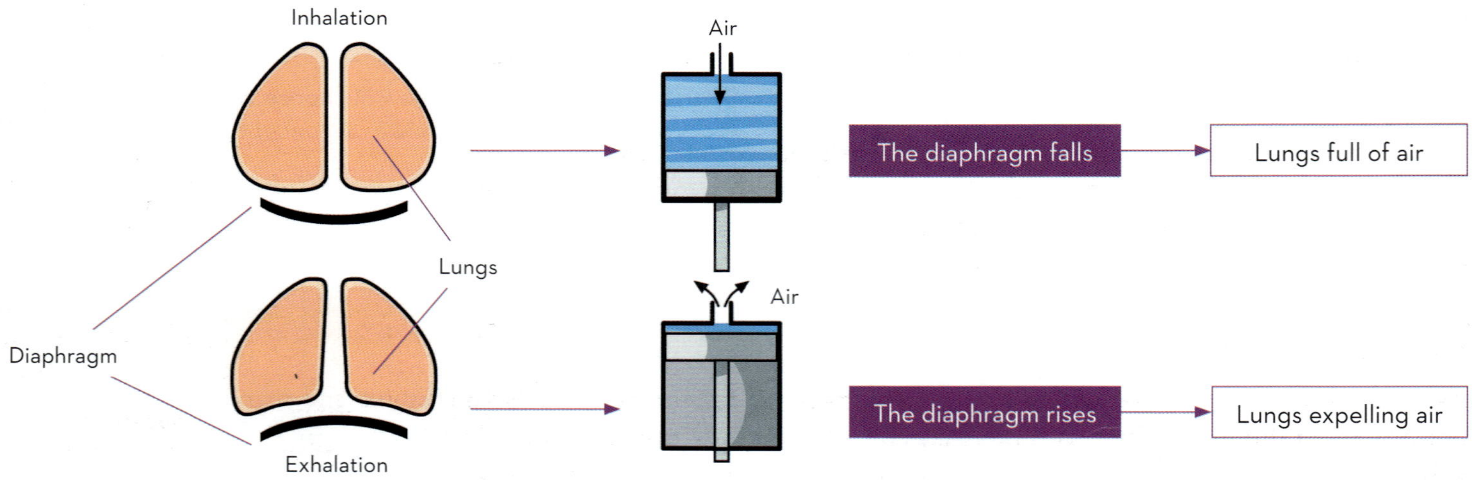

Figure 4.1.
The **diaphragm** pushes against the lower part of the lungs, expelling the air with greater pressure and continuity.

People who use their voice to sing or to talk in public have to control their breathing well. Good respiration allows the air that enters the body to leave it as sound, but without damaging any of the organs involved in the process.

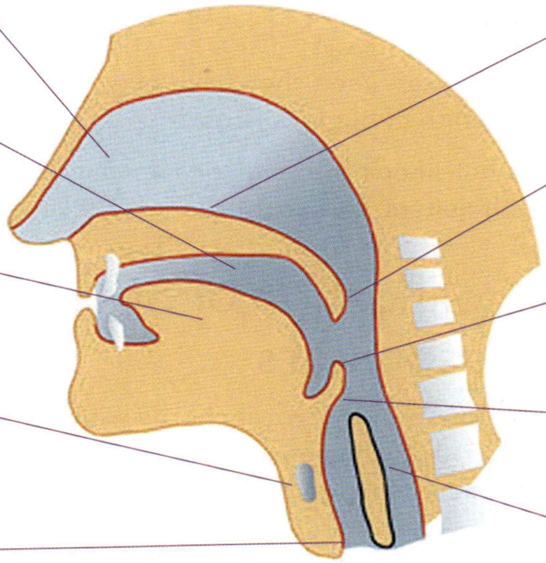

Figure 4.2.
Upper part of the respiratory system.

WORKSHEET

3. Download, make a list of words and match to Figure 4.2.
4. Search for videos about breathing on YouTube. You can write 'breathing techniques for singing' to find them. Practice what you learn from the videos with your classmates and teacher.

ACTIVITIES

1. **Inhale as much air as you can as quickly as possible. Did you notice that your shoulders rise? And that it was the upper part of your lungs that fill up with the most air?**
2. **Empty your lungs completely. Now breathe in slowly with your hand on your stomach. Try to make the air reach the bottom part of your lungs so that your stomach pushes your hand away.**

• Complete Breathing

As you saw in the previous activity, when we breathe we tend to fill only the upper part of the lungs. This does not take full advantage of ou- lung capacity. When singing, we must try to fill the entire lung space. First, we fill the lower part and then the upper part.

This is called *complete breathing* and it is essential to sing well. It is also beneficial to your health. However, we do not always have to fill our lungs completely because we do not always need that much air.

DID YOU KNOW?

Hiccups are caused by a sudden contraction of the diaphragm. This causes air to enter very quickly and the vocal chords to close. This is what makes the singular sound of hiccups.

1.2. The Production of Sound

Imagine a guitar. It produces sound when a force (in this case the guitarist's thumb) makes the strings vibrate.

The same thing happens with your voice. Pushed by the diaphragm, air flows from the lungs to the larynx. The larynx has two small tendons called the **vocal chords** (Figure 4.3). These tense and vibrate as the air passes, producing sound.

Just as guitars sound better when they have new, good quality strings, our voice depends on the state of our vocal chords.

Actions like smoking, not sleeping enough or screaming too much can damage them. Plus, unlike with guitars, we cannot change our vocal chords.

Figure 4.3.
Vocal chords.

1.3. The Amplification of Sound in the Resonators

We compared the vibration of the vocal chords with the strings on a guitar. Without a large resonance chamber, the sound of the strings would be weak and have poor timbre. The same thing happens with the voice: the weak sound produced in the vocal chords amplifies in the resonators in our body (Figure 4.4). These are basically the **facial cavities** (the hollow spaces in our face and head) and the chest (the **thoracic cavity**).

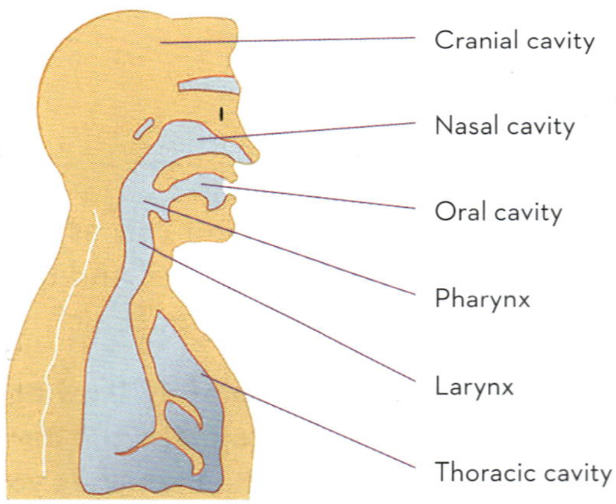

Figure 4.4.
The **resonators** give the voice its timbral quality and force of sound.

CURIOUS FACTS

Power without electricity

Have you ever been to the theatre or the opera? Did you notice that you can hear the actors or singers perfectly without them using a microphone or amplifier?

It is not a magic trick, it is simply because these people know how to use the resonators in their voice very well. This amplifies the sound naturally.

You can go to the **OLC activities** to watch interesting videos about this.

ACTIVITIES

3. Put one hand on your forehead and the other on your chest. Now sing a high sound then a low sound. What can you feel in each of your hands?

Notice how the high note produces a greater vibration in the hand on your forehead. When you sing the low note, the vibration is stronger in the hand on your chest.

This is because the resonators in your head influence the high notes more. The bone structure in your chest works more during the low notes.

2 Voice Training

Do you think singers are born or made? Sometimes we hear comments such as 'I have a terrible singing voice' or 'I have always sung really well.' This makes us think that either you have a voice or you do not. This is not always the case, as voice training can transform a mediocre voice into quite a good one.

But voice training has an added challenge. Unlike a musical instrument, we cannot see the vocal instrument and this makes the teacher's job more difficult. Voice training requires time and dedication.

When someone decides to train his/her voice, the first thing the singing teacher does is to analyse the situation and the possibilities. The first step is to determine the voice's **tessitura.** In other words, this is to see which set of notes the person's voice can emit without difficulty and with timbral quality.

RESOURCES WEB

The website has more information and data on tessitura.

WORKSHEET

5. Describe your favourite voices.
6. Organise the phrases to make the definition of tessitura:

   with timbral quality / set of notes / without difficulty / the person's voice can emit.

See the diagram to play with your partner in the OLC.

ACTIVITIES

4. Check your voice's tessitura.

- Using the middle C on the piano, sing the scale progressively upwards (from low to high). Write down the first note that is difficult for you to reach comfortably and clearly.
- Do the same again, but this time sing the scale progressively downwards, from the C to the low notes (*C, B, A*).

The range of notes between the two you wrote down is your tessitura. It is normal for it to be quite a small range. Do not get discouraged because your vocal range can increase by practising exercises like the ones in the *In Tune* section of this book.

Classical music, especially genres like *opera, zarzuela,* etc., require very powerful voices with a wide tessitura. These singers use the **vocal apparatus** and the **resonating chambers** to the best of their abilities to project their voice as much as possible. You can hear their voices well in a theatre. We say they have good voice projection and a wide vocal range. But these voices do not always adapt well stylistically to other genres, such as *pop* or *jazz*. This type of music uses a more natural voice or sometimes needs a specific type of timbre.

Figure 4.5.
Montserrat Caballé. One of the great voices of opera.

ACTIVITIES

5. Listen to two excerpts from the famous song *Hijo de la Luna* by the group Mecano. The first is the original and the second is a version by Montserrat Caballé (Figure 4.5). Are the voices trained to project well or do you think they are more natural voices? Which version do you prefer? Why?

> **DID YOU KNOW?**
>
> In the 1st century the famous orator Quintilian classified the voice in his publication *Institutes of Oratory*. There is quantity (large, medium, small) and quality (clear, dark, sweet, rich, etc.).

> **RESOURCES WEB**
>
> The website contains further information on the *castrati* and there are interesting activities about the castrati in the OLC.

> **DID YOU KNOW?**
>
> The practice of castrating boys before their voice broke began in the 16th century. It aimed to preserve their high voices into adulthood, but seems like an aberration to us now.

3 Types of Voices: Classifying Voices

Voices are traditionally classified according to their tessitura. These classifications began to be defined in the Renaissance. They are mainly used for vocal genres such as *opera* and *zarzuela*.

Classifying a voice properly is important. If people try to sing in the wrong tessitura, they can suffer irreversible damage to their vocal chords.

The simplest and most common classification divides male and female singers. Each gender has subdivisions from the lowest to the highest vocal range as shown in the tables below:

Male Voices		Female Voices
Tenors	**High** ↑	Sopranos
Baritones		Mezzo-sopranos
Basses	**Low**	Contraltos

Children's voices are called *trebles* and they have a tessitura similar to women. During adolescence, the voice changes or *breaks*.

The vocal chords become longer in boys than in girls. The voice drops an octave in boys and two or three tones in girls.

ACTIVITIES

6. Listen to the highest and lowest voices of women and men and try to guess the type of voice that you hear. Fill in the chart in the OLC.

Some men manage to sing with the tessitura of a woman using the *falsetto* register of their voice. They have to train specially to sing like this. These singers are called **countertenors.**

Many singers in pop and heavy metal also use this falsetto to achieve vocal effects. However, they are not called countertenors; this term is mainly used for opera singers.

Pitch is another aspect that requires careful attention in singing. An incorrect voice classification can make the singer sound forced and even out of tune on some notes.

On other occasions there are voices with great power and quality, but the singers are **tone deaf** and cannot make good use of their vocal capacity.

You have probably heard this when someone sings karaoke with a voice that has a nice sound but is really out of tune.

CURIOUS FACTS

A happy (but out of tune) birthday!

Have you noticed that when people sing *Happy Birthday* they often sing out of tune? Do you know why? It is a problem with **vocal range.**

The song rises a lot in the second part. If they start singing very high, it is difficult to reach the higher notes that come later. They are outside most people's tessitura. That is why they sing **out of tune.**

ACTIVITIES

7. **Do you want to see what happens when you sing *Happy Birthday*? Sing the song starting from the different pitches your teacher gives you.**

8. **Timeless voices.**

   The photos below show three singers with very special voices. They are now part of music history for having such singular timbres and vocal capacities. Investigate and match each photo with a style of music and with each excerpt of the listening.

RESOURCES WEB

If you want to learn to play *Happy Birthday*, you can find the score on the website.

Figure 4.6.
Camarón de la Isla.

Figure 4.7.
Ella Fitzgerald.

Figure 4.8.
Maria Callas.

4 Vocal Groupings

As we saw in Unit 3, instrumentalists form different groups to play music. The same is done with voices. The most characteristic vocal formation is the *choir*. Perhaps you have sung in one at school or in your neighbourhood. Choirs vary in how many members they have. When there are few voices, they are called **chamber choirs.** Choirs with both men and women's voices are called **mixed choirs** and this is the most common formation.

The singers are normally separated into four groups according to their tessitura. These are called *choral voice parts*. Women sing the *soprano* and *alto* choral parts and the men sing the *tenor* and *bass* parts.

The director decides the position of the singers, but sometimes it depends on the stage and the acoustics of the place where the choir is singing. One of the most commonly used is shown below:

Figure 4.9.
Coro Discantus during a performance.

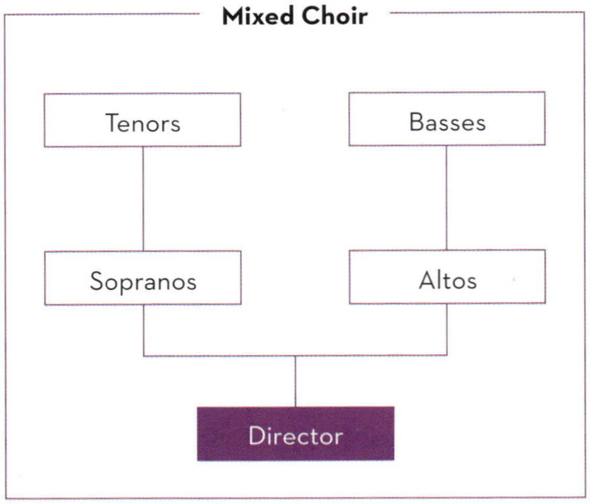

There are also exclusively **male or female choirs** and **treble choirs** (with children's voices).

ACTIVITIES

9. **A choir is self-sufficient and can sing many types of music without the need for instruments. This is called *a cappella* singing. Listen to these two musical excerpts:**

The first one is sung by a famous English choir, **The King's Singers.** There are six male singers singing a song by **The Beatles** and they even imitate the instruments with their voices. They are men, but observe that there are voices with a female tessitura (in this case two countertenors).

In the second piece, the mixed choir **The Swingle Singers** performs a Scottish melody entitled ***Loch Lomond.*** The singing has a 'harmonic warmth' that only comes from voices.

WORKSHEET

7. Make a list of the main choirs you know and fill in the chart in the OLC.
8. Download and complete the sentences.

DID YOU KNOW?

Many of the great composers in the history of music, like **J. Sebastian Bach** o **Mozart**, sang in church or cathedral choirs when they were young. This contributed significantly to their musical education.

5 Auditorium: Opera

A. The Facts

Around 1600 a musical style called *opera* developed. It aimed to imitate the ancient Greek and Roman civilizations.

Over the next few centuries, this genre became more and more important. Eventually, it became the most popular secular (not religious) musical genre. For the great composers, creating an opera was a sign of prestige and a good source of income.

An **opera** is a theatrical work with singing. It requires lots of people and resources to perform it on stage. These include the orchestra, the soloists, the chorus, the dancers, the costumes and the scenery, among other aspects.

Opera has influenced other musical styles such as **Broadway musicals** (*Cats*, *The Phantom of the Opera, West Side Story*) and even rock, for example the famous **rock opera** *Jesus Christ Superstar*.

There are **opera theatres** all around the world, including some very famous ones in certain countries. In Spain we have two very important ones: the Teatro Real in Madrid and the Liceu in Barcelona.

B. The Music

In an opera we find different **musical parts.** Listen to the following fragments. They illustrate some of these parts.

The **overture** is an orchestral piece with no singing voices. It is a musical introduction to the opera. It normally begins with the curtain down. Listen to an excerpt from the overture to the opera *The Barber of Seville* by **Rossini**.

The **recitatives** are the parts used to tell the story or move the action forward. They are sung dialogues between the characters. They usually have a very simple musical accompaniment. The fragment you will hear belongs to the opera *The Marriage of Figaro* by **Mozart**. Two servants talk about their master's complicated love life.

An **aria** is a song for soloists. Along with the choruses, the arias are the audience's favourite parts. They tend to be very beautiful and spectacular as well as demonstrating all the vocal qualities of the main singers. They usually express the characters' feelings (love, suffering, happiness , etc.). You will hear the aria *O mio babbino caro* from the opera *Gianni Schicchi* by the composer **Giacomo Puccini.**

The **choruses** are sung by lots of the characters in the opera. They move around the stage and then sing together in certain parts of the performance. Choruses are usually very beautiful and emotive. Many of them are famous, including the one you will hear. You probably recognise the music entitled *Va pensiero* from the opera *Nabucco* by **Verdi.**

DID YOU KNOW?

In the 17th century a new theatrical-musical genre developed in Spain called *zarzuela*. It has similar characteristics to opera but **spoken parts** alternate with the sung parts. In opera everything is sung. You can see an excerpt of the zarzuela *La Dolores* on the RESOURCES WEB.

RESOURCES WEB

On the website you can watch a scene from the musical *Cats*. You can also learn more about the different operatic parts explained in this section.

WORKSHEET

9. See the glossary: Useful expressions in regard to rhythm.

6 A Lot of Rhythm

In this lesson you are going to work with *semiquavers*:

Ti ri ti ri

Play the following exercises by tapping your hands on your knees, alternating your right and left hands. Then play them with the recording in the resources.

Exercise 1

Exercise 2

Practise this polyrhythm with two hands:

Exercise 3

Previously we saw how the instruments in a drum kit are represented on a stave. Now we will transform our body into a drum kit. We will assign each instrument to a part of the body: the *bass* will be your right foot; the *snare*, your left hand (on your thigh); and the *ride cymbal*, your right hand.

Practise the following drum patterns using body percussion. Then play with the recording.

Exercise 4

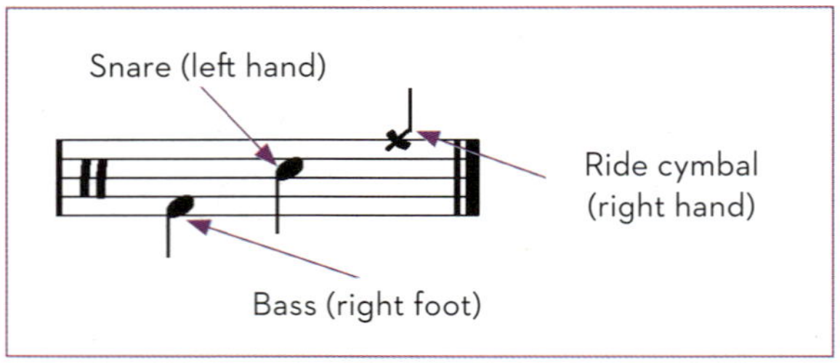

7 In Tune

A. Train Your Voice

In this exercise we will combine the task of increasing your vocal range (from Unit 2) with the work on melodic jumps (from Unit 3).

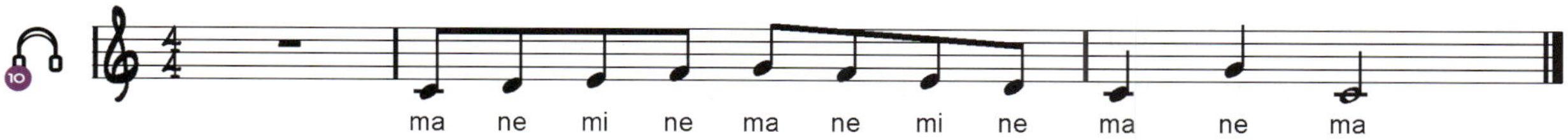

B. Reading Music

We are going to add the low *A* and *B* notes to the ones we have already worked on. Observe that the note A requires an additional line below the standard stave. Mark a beat and say the name of the notes (without singing):

In the following piece, you are going to sing all the notes you have just read in the score exercise. We have another challenge for you, too! Sing the repetition of the piece at a faster tempo. This requires greater skill to sing in tune and to say the correct name of each note. Good luck!

C. Interpretive Exercise

DID YOU KNOW?

The vowels **e** and **i** facilitate the correct placement of high notes.

WORKSHEET

10. If you want to train your voice and sing with your friends better, remember the page useful expressions in regard to singing.

Figure 4.10.

Some people in certain cultures can sing two or more notes at the same time. This harmonic sound is called *overtone singing*.

WORKSHEET

11. See the glossary: Useful expressions in regard to playing the recorder.

8 Move Your Fingers

With the practice from previous units, we are ready to learn new notes and their positions. Learning and practising these notes will enable us to play more complex melodies. It is time to discover C *sharp* and D *sharp*.

Practise the following exercises. The resources for this unit include these accompaniments:

Figure 4.11.
Sitar. Indo-Arabic instrument.

Figure 4.12.
Bansuri. Traditional Indian flute.

- Accompaniments for Exercises 1, 2 and 3: percussion and bowed string section in the accompaniment. In the melody we have the *oboe, flute* and *bassoon.*
- Accompaniments for Exercises 4, 5 and 6: you will hear a curious background of Indian music. This includes typical instruments from India: the *sitar* (Figure 4.11), *bansuri* (Figure 4.12) and *tablas*.

Exercise 1. *C' D'*

Exercise 2

Exercise 3

Exercise 4

Exercise 5

Exercise 6

9 Concert

On this occasion our concert piece is *Druida*. The composition spans various styles and cannot be defined as just one.

It is a melodic composition, along the lines of a soundtrack. It includes elements of Celtic music, with instruments such as the *Celtic harp* (Figure 4.13), *bodram*, and *tin whistle* (Figure 4.14). It also has instruments used in symphony orchestras: *violins, violas, cellos, double basses* and the *English horn*. We will look at these instruments more closely in other units.

Figure 4.13.
Celtic harp. Plucked string instrument. It is smaller than the classic harp.

Druida

14 15

Music: José Luis Salas

Figure 4.14.
Tin whistle. Traditional brass wind instrument in Celtic cultures.

Celtic music combines several musical genres in the folkloric music of Western Europe. We now use this term for music that includes rhythmic and melodic elements from this tradition, but it may not be purely Celtic.

Some of the most commonly used instruments in this music are: the *violin, bagpipes, accordion, whistle, bodhran* and *Celtic harp*, among others.

WORKSHEET

12. What are the main instruments in Celtic music?
13. Search pictures on the Internet of the instruments that are not in the book and videos of Celtic music performance.

10 Relaxing with Music

You probably use music to relax, cheer you up or inspire you. In this unit you will experiment with a guided relaxation using music.

Before we begin, follow these instructions:

DID YOU KNOW?

There is a discipline called **music therapy**. It uses music to help people feel well.

A. Breathing

Breathe through your nose. Try to make it as relaxed and comfortable as possible.

ACTIVITIES

10. To learn to control your breathing better, do this exercise. Inhale through your nose and mentally count 1-2. Exhale through your nose counting 1-2-3-4. When you feel comfortable, try counting to 4 as you inhale and to 8 as you exhale. Observe how this exercise helps you to relax.

B. Position

For the relaxation to be more effective sit up straight in your chair without crossing your legs and rest your hands on your thighs. If you have enough space and some mats, you can do this lying down. Lie on your back and let your arms rest on the floor with your palms facing upwards.

ACTIVITIES

11. Close your eyes and listen carefully to this guided relaxation. At the end, spend a few minutes writing about how you feel in your Workbook. What did this music inspire in you?

WORKSHEET

14. How did you feel while doing the guided relaxation?

Share with your partner and write your feelings.

Download and print the worksheet you will find in the OLC to complete the concept map of the unit.

The v ... instrument

- Vocal a ...
  - The p ... of the b ... that participate in producing the v ...
- P ... or phases
  - **Respiration** (l ... and d ...).
  - The **p ...** of sound (vocal c ...).
  - The **amplification** of sound (r ...).

Voice t ...

- Determining the **t ... of the voice** (the s ... of notes where the sound is e ... e ... and with good t ...).
- **Voice p ...** (powerful voices that make the b ... use of the v ... apparatus and resonators).

T ... of voices: Classifying voices

M ... Voices		F ... Voices
T ...	High	S ...
B ...		M ... sopranos
B ...	L ...	C ...

* T ... voices (children's voices).
* C ... (men who sing in a woman's tessitura using the highest part of their vocal range, commonly called *f ...*).

Vocal g ...

- C ...
  - **C ... choir** (small number of voices).
  - **M ... choir** (men and women).
  - **Treble choir** (only ch ... 's voices).
  - * Singing *a c ...* (only voices, without instruments).

FINAL ACTIVITIES

1. Explain the following concepts in your Workbook:

a) Complete breathing.

b) Tessitura.

c) Voice projection.

d) Treble voices.

e) Facial resonators.

f) *A capella.*

g) Countertenors.

h) Mixed choir.

2. Why is it necessary to classify a voice correctly?

3. In your Workbook order the following voices from low to high. Name two other types of voices not included in this list.

tenor	bass	contralto
mezzo-soprano	baritone	soprano

4. Draw a diagram showing the most common position for the different voice types in a mixed choir. How would you place them if they were all in single file in a semicircle?

5. Imagine you are at the opera. Complete the following sentences in your Workbook. Remember the parts of the opera we discussed in the *Auditorium* section.

a) The curtain is down and the orchestra plays in the darkness. You are listening to ... .

b) A young man sings a beautiful melody suffering from a lost love. You are listening to ... .

c) A group of pilgrims sing as they walk. You are listening to ... .

d) A singer narrates the situation of one of the characters in the story. You are listening to ... .

6. On the RESOURCES WEB you can watch an excerpt of a very famous opera: *La bohème*. There is also more information about it. After watching it and reading about it, answer the following questions in your Workbook:

a) Who composed *La bohème*?

b) What are the names of the two main characters?

c) Write a brief summary of the opera's storyline or plot.

7. **Search on the internet and classify the voices of these famous opera singers:**

   a) Luciano Pavarotti.

   b) Ainhoa Arteta.

   c) Elisabeth Schwarzkopf.

   d) Teresa Berganza.

   e) Plácido Domingo.

   f) Hermann Prey.

   g) Alfredo Kraus.

   h) Kiri Te Kanawa.

   i) Walter Berry.

8. **You are going to be journalists. Form work groups. Each group must interview singers from a youth choir to obtain the answers to the following questions:**

   a) Why do you like singing in a choir?

   b) How many people are in your choir?

   c) How often do you rehearse?

   d) What type of music do you sing?

   The groups will share their answers in class. You can find youth choirs by asking local schools if they have a choir or by searching on the internet for local choir associations.

FINAL PROJECT

1. With your group of classmates design a poster or a digital poster with advice for good vocal hygiene. You can write 10 ways to take care of your voice using sentences and/or graphics.

2. You can visit some websites on the internet. We recommend typing 'vocal hygiene' into Google.

   Do an oral presentation showing your posters.

   Have a class discussion. Talk about your vocal hygiene habits. Decide if you think any of your habits could be damaging your vocal health.

3. Assess your other classmates' posters and presentations.

5 MUSICAL INSTRUMENTS

In previous units we studied some of the basic elements of music. But musicians need musical instruments to reproduce music. As a painter needs brushes or a sculptor a chisel, musicians need musical instruments to reproduce sound.

Musical instruments existed since very early times. The first were very primitive, but over time they improved to have the appearance we recognise today.

In this unit you will learn to visually and aurally identify the most important musical instruments, how they produce sound, their classification and the most common instrumental ensembles.

Contents

WORK ON THE TEXT

Download the worksheet 'Work on the text' and fill in the gaps activity.

WARM UP

1. Think about the instruments you see in your Music classroom, the ones you have at home or those you know about. Classify those instruments in groups: wind, string, percussion and electronic. You can use the chart in the OLC.
2. Search for some virtual instruments on the internet.
3. Download an application of some virtual instruments on your mobile phone.
4. Play some of the instruments.
5. The teacher will play some of the instruments you have in your classroom for you.

FIND A CLASSMATE

1. Compare your classmate's instruments and complete your chart of instruments.
2. Share your virtual instrument apps with your classmates.
3. Try to play their instruments. What do you like most?

KEYWORDS

Download and print the activities that will guide you through the essential vocabulary of this unit.

1 Musical Instruments

Every musical instrument has its own ***timbre*** or characteristic *colour*, so the same piece of music may sound very different depending on the instrument that plays it. It is very important for a composer to know about the *timbres* and *expressive* qualities of them.

For example, think about the music we hear in films. String music accompanies many romantic scenes, but in war scenes the use of brass and percussion is frequent.

ACTIVITIES

1. Listen to the same piece of music played by a *violin*, a *saxophone* and a *xylophone* and observe how the use of one or another musical instrument influences the final result.

The timbre of a musical instrument depends on many factors: the way it emits sound, the material it is made of, its shape, its size, etc. Depending on *how they produce sound*, we classify musical instruments into different instrument families:

- **String instruments:** These produce sound by the vibration of a taut string. Example: the *violin*.
- **Wind instruments:** We make sound by blowing air into them. This vibrates the air inside a tube. They are divided into woodwind and brass. Example: the *trumpet*.
- **Percussion instruments:** We make sound by striking or shaking the instrument. Example: the *timpani*.

Another type is the **electronic instruments.** These use electricity to make the instrument sound. They need an amplifier. Examples: the *electric guitar*, the *bass guitar*, the *synthesiser*, etc.

ACTIVITIES

2. Make a list in your workbook with the names of all the musical instruments that you know. According to how they produce sound, classify them as string, wind or percussion.

Next we will study each of the instrument families to know more about all these instruments.

WORKSHEET

1. Start to make a glossary about actions or verbs related to instruments. Search for these words in the unit.

   See the OLC to fill in the chart.

1.1. String Instruments

These produce sound through the vibration of taut strings. They also have a sound board to amplify the sound. There are three types according to how we obtain the sound: *bowed*, *plucked* and *struck*.

Figure 5.1.
Double bass.

A. Bowed String Instruments

We obtain sound by rubbing the strings with a bow. From the highest-pitched to the lowest-pitched, they are the following: violin, viola, cello and double bass.

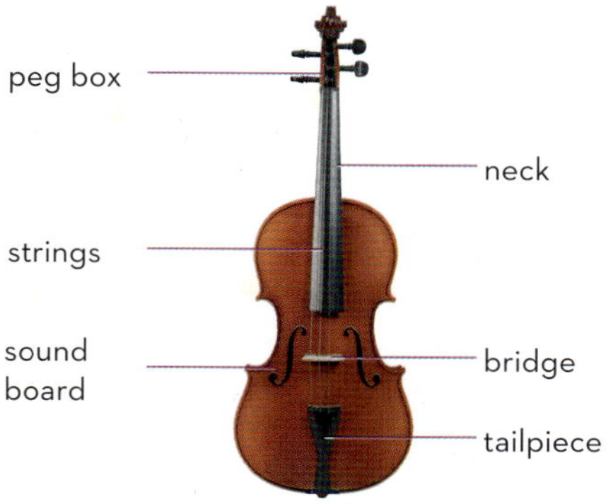

Figure 5.4.
Violin.

Figure 5.3.
Viola.

Figure 5.2.
Cello.

WORKSHEET

2. Download matching activities in the OLC.
3. See the OLC activity on a BBC video.

ACTIVITIES

16 **6. You will hear the bowed string instruments in a random order. Try to guess the order of appearance.**

B. Plucked String Instruments

We obtain sound by touching the strings with our fingers or a plectrum. These instruments include the *guitar* (Figure 5.5) and the harp (Figure 5.6).

C. Struck String Instruments

We obtain sound by striking the strings. An example of this type of instruments is the *piano* (Figure 5.7). The pianist presses the keys to make hammers strike the strings. These strings are in the sound board.

Figure 5.5.
The **guitar** adapts to very diverse styles, such as classical, pop or flamenco music.

Figure 5.6.
The **harp** has strings in different colours so that the musician can locate the notes more easily.

Figure 5.7.
Cristofori made the first **piano** in 1709. Its original name was pianoforte, because it can make sounds of different intensities.

WORKSHEET

4. See the OLC activity on a BBC video.
5. Unscramble and find the odd word out:

   xosa / parh / linvio / lloce / tufle / eobo / ssoonba / tarigu / nopai.

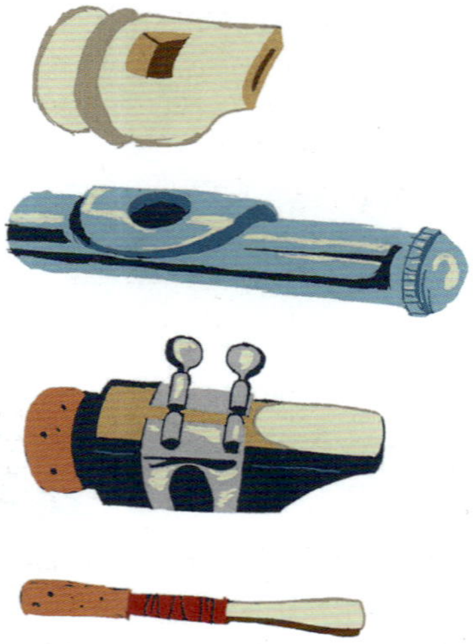

Figure 5.8.
Woodwind mouthpieces.

1.2. Wind Instruments

These produce sound through the vibration of the air inside the instrument tube. We can group them into woodwind and brass instruments. This classification can be a little confusing because now some of the instruments of the woodwind family are made of metal (for example, the *transverse flute* and the *saxophone*). What really determines the sound is the type of *mouthpiece* (Figure 5.8) the instrument has.

A. Woodwind

There are three types of instruments according to their mouthpiece:

- **Flutes:** The air vibrates when it hits a hole with a sharp edge. This occurs in the *recorder* (Figure 5.9) and the *transverse flute* (Figure 5.10).
- **Single-reed instruments:** Vibrating air produces sound when it hits a reed or strip of cane in the mouthpiece of the instrument. For example: the *clarinet* (Figure 5.11) and the *saxophone* (Figure 5.12).
- **Double-reed instruments:** Air is pushed through two reeds to vibrate and produce sound. The *oboe* (Figure 5.13) and the *bassoon* (Figure 5.14) have this type of mouthpiece.

ACTIVITIES

3. Listen to how the following woodwind instruments sound in a random order. Try to guess the order of appearance. Make your own matching activity on woodwind instruments and play with your partner.

Flutes

Figure 5.9.
The instrument you play in class is a plastic model of the **recorder**.

Figure 5.10.
Transverse flute.

Single-reed instruments

Figure 5.11.
Clarinet.

Figure 5.12.
Saxophone.

Double-reed instruments

Figure 5.13.
Oboe.

Figure 5.14.
Bassoon.

B. Brass

These are made with metal. The tube of the instrument is folded or coiled around itself to make it more functional. (If we could 'uncoil' a *tuba*, its total length would be 3.65 m.)

The pitch of the sound depends on the air pressure the musician produces on the mouthpiece and a system of valves and pistons. (Instead of pistons, the *trombone* uses a moving slide.)

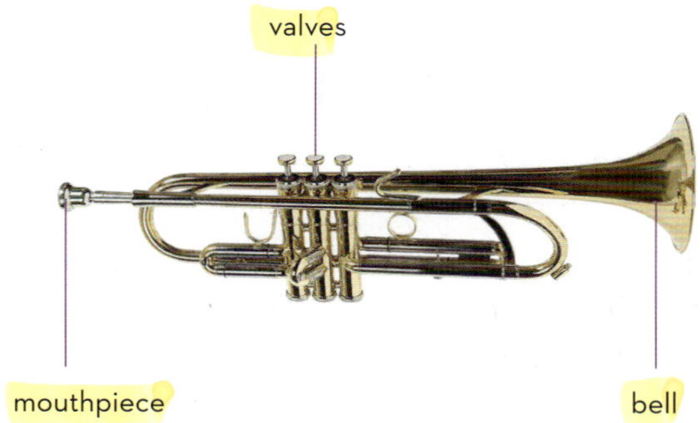

Figure 5.15.
Trumpet.

Figure 5.16.
French horn.

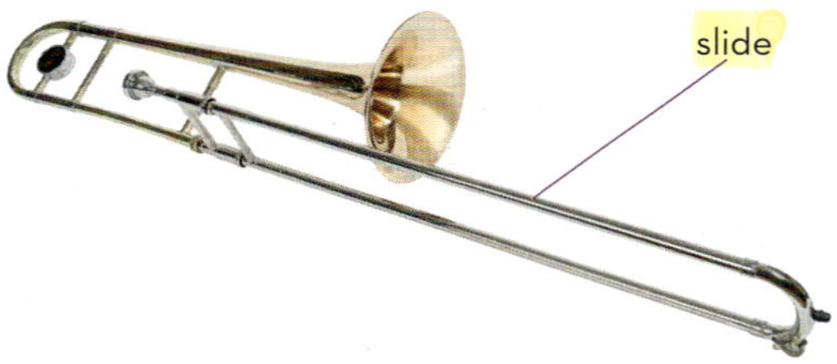

Figure 5.17.
Trombone.

Figure 5.18.
Tuba.

CURIOUS FACTS

A musician can insert a **mute** into the bell of a brass instrument to modify its sound.

WORKSHEET

6. Make your own matching activity on brass instruments and share with your partner.
7. See the OLC activity on a BBC video.

RESOURCES WEB

You can find more information about woodwind and brass instruments on the website.

ACTIVITIES

4. Listen to the following recording of these brass instruments in a random order. Try to guess the order of appearance.

C. The Organ and Other Wind Instruments

The **organ** (Figure 5.19) is a wind instrument with a keyboard. It has a system of tubes of different lengths. In the past, manual bellows provided the air. Now an electric pump does this. It has a large variety of timbres.

Other wind instruments include the accordion, harmonica or mouth organ, etc.

Figure 5.19.
Organ.

1.3. Percussion Instruments

These instruments produce sound when we strike them (like the *drum*), crash them together (like *cymbals*), shake them (for example, *maracas*) or scrape them (like the *guiro*). We can divide them into two groups:

- ***Pitched percussion:*** These instruments can produce sounds with a specific pitch, or note. They include: the *timpani* (Figure 5.20), *xylophone, glockenspiel, tubular bells* or *chimes* (Figure 5.21), *marimba* (Figure 5.22), etc.

Figure 5.20.
Timpani.

Figure 5.22.
Tubular bells
or chimes.

Figure 5.21.
Marimba.

- ***Unpitched percussion:*** These instruments do not produce specific pitches. For example: the *bass drum* (Figure 5.23), *snare drum* (Figure 5.24), and *cymbals* (Figure 5.25). In other styles, instruments like the *bongos, maracas, claves*, etc., are common.

Figure 5.23.
Bass drum.

Figure 5.25.
Snare drum.

Figure 5.24.
Cymbals.

RESOURCES WEB

You can find more information about percussion instruments on the website.

WORKSHEET

8. Make your own matching activity on percussion instruments and play with your partner.
9. See the OLC activity on a BBC video.

ACTIVITIES

5. Listen to the recording and try to discover which percussion instruments sound. Also decide if they are pitched percussion or unpitched percussion. Can you say which one of them is not typical of the symphony orchestra?

2 Instrumental Ensembles

2.1. Symphony Orchestra

This instrumental ensemble has the largest number of instrumentalists. Originally there were string instruments and some woodwind and brass instruments. Over time, their number and variety increased by also adding percussion instruments.

The placement of the instruments on stage is to find a balance of timbres and sounds. We group the instruments in their families, with the louder ones farther from the audience. There is also a contrast between the high-pitched instruments (on the left) and the low-pitched instruments (on the right).

WORKSHEET

10. You can also do other fun activities in the OLC.

DID YOU KNOW?

The origin of the term **orchestra** is Greek. It was the place of the theatre where the musicians sat.

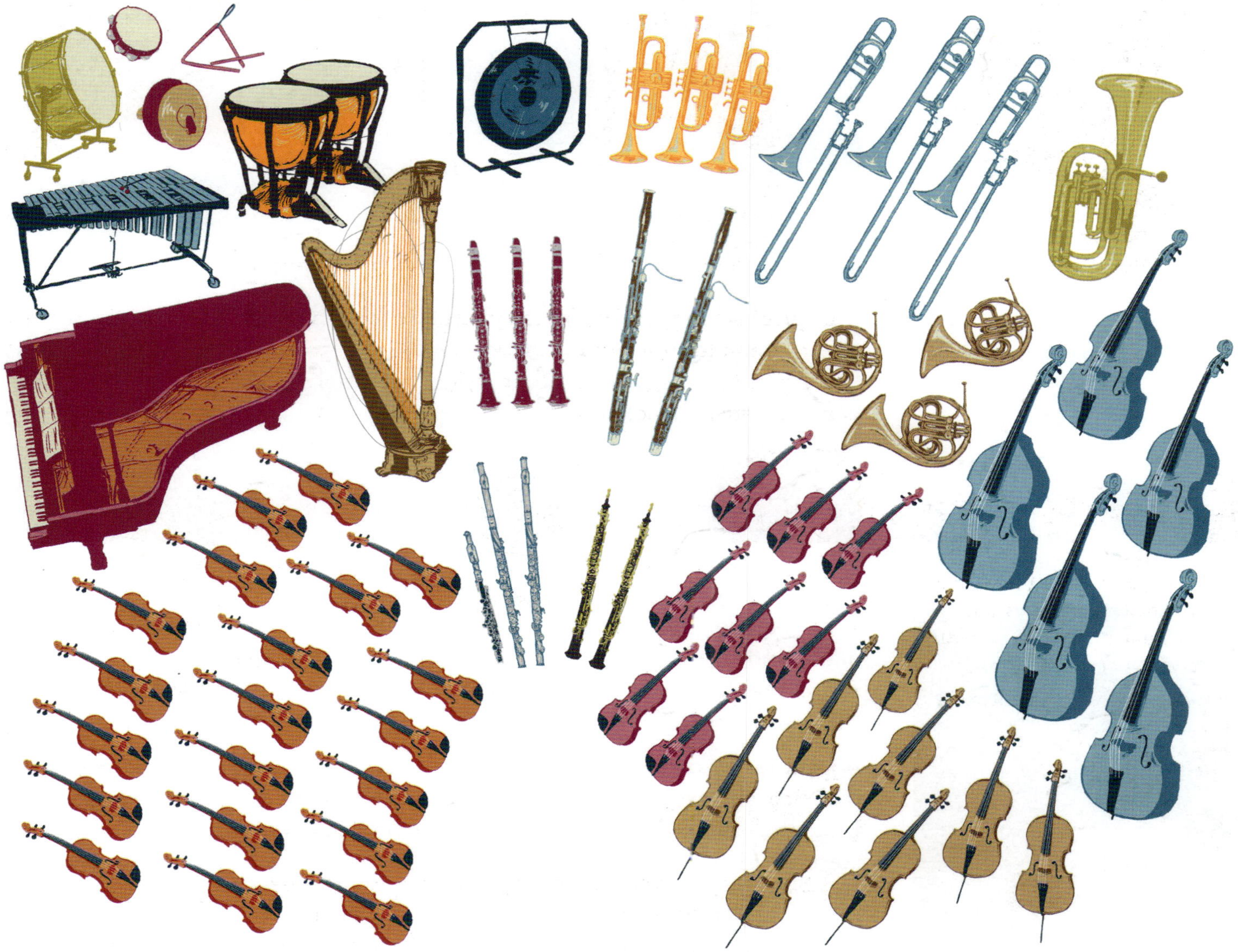

Figure 5.26.
The symphony orchestra is the most representative musical ensemble of Western art music.

DID YOU KNOW?

Currently, the first violin is the *leader* and substitutes the conductor when he/she is not there. The most important function is to play an A note with the instrument before the beginning of a concert so that all the orchestra tunes to this note.

WORKSHEET

11. Make a jumbled word game with all the names of the instruments in the orchestra. Every group makes this with every section of the orchestra.

    Swap your games and play them.

    Who is going to win?

The instruments of the orchestra, grouped by sections, are:

- **String instruments:** *violins, violas, cellos* and *double basses*. Sometimes other instruments appear as soloists, like the *piano, harp* or *guitar*.
- **Woodwind instruments:** *transverse flutes, oboes, clarinets* and *bassoons*.
- **Brass instruments:** *trumpets, French horns, trombones* and *tubas*.
- **Percussion instruments:** *timpani, xylophone, tubular bells* or *chimes, bass drum, cymbals,* etc.

The orchestra formed at the end of the 17th century and the beginning of the 18th century. It has become larger over time.

Figure 5.27.
Symphony orchestra.

Figure 5.28.
Leonard Bernstein, an important orchestra conductor.

The figure of the **orchestra conductor** is very important. He/she coordinates and directs all the instrumentalists. He/she knows how the musical score should sound and makes his/her instrument, the orchestra, play it that way.

An orchestra conductor has a lot of musical culture and knows about the technical and expressive possibilities of each instrument. His/her mission is also to control the pitch of the entire group, indicate when the instrumentalists start to play, mark the tempo, indicate the character of the music, etc. The right hand moves the *baton* and the left hand indicates the differences in the expression of the song.

Great conductors of the 20th century include Herbert von Karajan, Leonard Bernstein (Figure 5.28), Claudio Abbado and Daniel Baremboim.

2.2. Chamber Music Ensembles

These are different types of smaller groups of instruments, with fewer musicians. Their names depend on the number of instruments in them: *duet, trio, quartet* (Figure 5.29), *quintet, chamber orchestra*, etc.

The *string quartet,* formed by two violins, a viola and a cello, was very important in the development of music history.

WORKSHEET

12. Make a mind map with the main names of the chamber music ensembles.
    a) Search for other interesting videos showing these ensembles on YouTube and share them in class.
    b) Make your own mind map with other ensembles.

Figure 5.29.
Picture of a string quartet.

2.3. Other Ensembles

- *Band:* instrumental ensemble composed of wind and percussion instruments.
- *Rock band:* composed of the *electric guitar, bass guitar* and *drum set*. Sometimes there are keyboards.
- Others: *trumpet and drum band, rondalla, plucked string orchestra, military band* (Figure 5.30), etc.

Figure 5.30.
Picture of a military band.

3 Other Instruments

In this unit we studied the most common musical instruments. Now we will learn about other types of instruments, like the instruments we use in classrooms to learn about music and typical instruments of other counties and cultures.

WORKSHEET

13. Who was Carl Orff? Search for information and share it with your classmates.
14. Download the worksheet about school instruments in the OLC and do the quiz.

3.1. School Instruments

Most instruments in music classrooms are *Orff instruments* (Figure 5.31). The composer and educator **Carl Orff** (1895-1982) used these for teaching music. They are mainly percussion instruments. Their technique is much easier than with professional instruments.

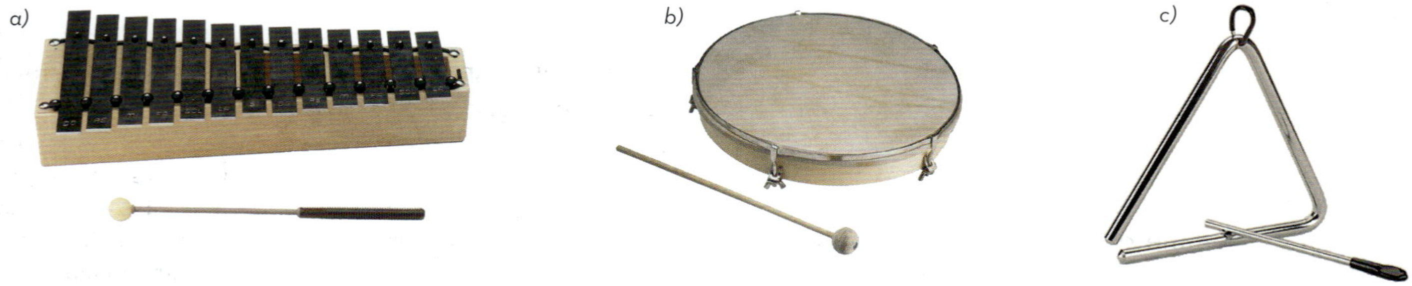

Figure 5.31.

Common instruments in the classroom: *a)* glockenspiel, *b)* tambourine, *c)* triangle.

WORKSHEET

15. Write all the world instruments you know. Open some links to interesting videos and find out more about your favourite ones. Share them with your partner.

3.2. Instruments of the World

These instruments are typical of a certain culture, country or region (Figure 5.32). In the book you will see information about some of them, because they accompany the pieces in the sections *Move Your Fingers* and *Concert*. Here are just some of them:

Figure 5.32.

Representation of some popular instruments of the world: *a)* alphorn (Switzerland), *b)* gamelan (Indonesia), *c)* *steel drums* (Caribbean).

4 Auditorium: Traditional African Music

A. The Facts

Music is present in any cultural manifestation of our planet. But in Africa, music has a more intense presence than in Europe.

In the area from the Sahara to the south of the continent, music and dance have a fundamental importance in different acts. These acts include funerals, weddings, preparation for hunting rituals, birth celebrations, communicating with ancestors or even spontaneously at any time of the day.

One important fact is that you don't need a stage or to be an excellent musician to make music in Africa. They make music simply to have fun and interact socially.

So we can say that for Africans, music is a vital way of communicating. Any moment and almost any place are ideal for many Africans to start singing, playing an instrument or dancing.

African music has a great variety of instruments, all of them handmade. You already know some of them, because we saw them in other sections of our book. We complete this information with the following:

- **Sanza** or **mbira:** This instrument sounds when a series of strips of metal or wood vibrates (Figure 5.33).
- **Kora:** a string instrument with a calabash for a sound board (Figure 5.34).
- **Tama drum:** This is called the *talking drum* because the pressure in the strings can regulate its tone (Figure 5.35).

Figure 5.33.
Sanza or **mbira.**

WORKSHEET

16. Cooperative writing/listening. Are you a good writer or a good listener? See the OLC activity about African music.
    What group is going to cooperate better and win?

B. The Music 5

For the Western world, African music is very exotic and attractive. Listen to some of its most characteristic elements:

- The percussion instruments play rich polyrhythms.
- The instruments are very different from those we use in European music, like the sanza you hear now.
- The peculiar use of voices with their 'captivating' character and typical nasal sound.

This music influenced many musical styles, like Latin music, and fused with very distant styles, like classical music. In this final piece, you can hear the song *Kayama*. It is from the musical project **Adiemus**. African voices mix with musical backgrounds of a classical orchestra.

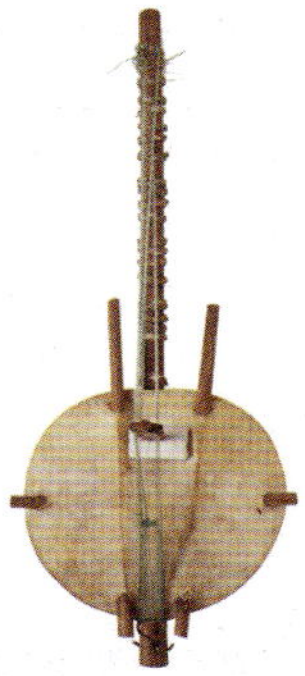

Figure 5.34.
Kora.

Figure 5.35.
Tama drum.

5 A Lot of Rhythm

WORKSHEET

17. See the glossary: useful expressions in regard to rhythm.

This lesson introduces a new rhythmic formula: *a dotted crotchet* and a *quaver*.

Remember the dot is half the value of the note it accompanies. So:

If ♩ = 1 beat, ♩. = 1 ½ beats and ♩. ♪ = 2 beats

Do the following rhythm exercises by clapping your hands or tapping your knees, alternating hands. You can also use rhythm syllables. Then do them with the recording:

Exercise 1

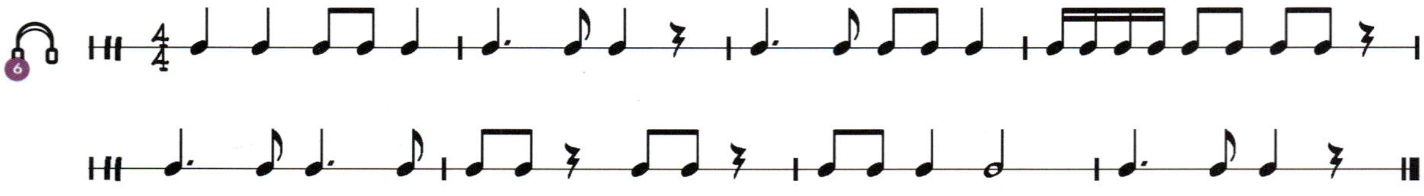

Exercise 2

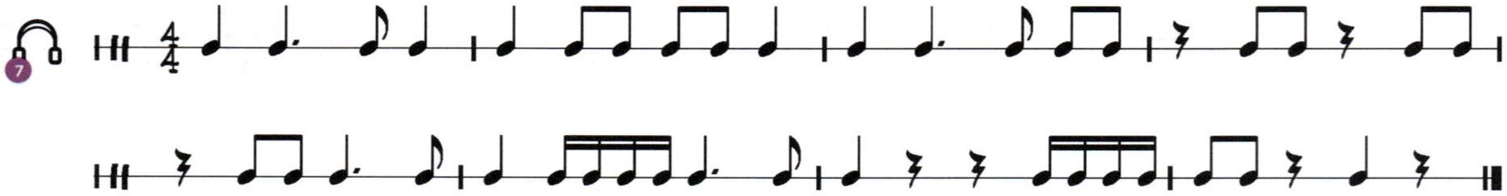

Practise this polyrhythm by tapping both hands on your knees. You can also do it with *bongos:*

Exercise 3

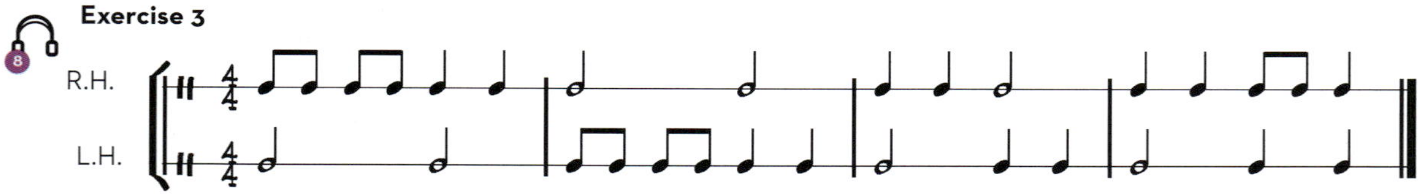

Practise the following *drum patterns* with body percussion. Then play them with the recording.

Exercise 4

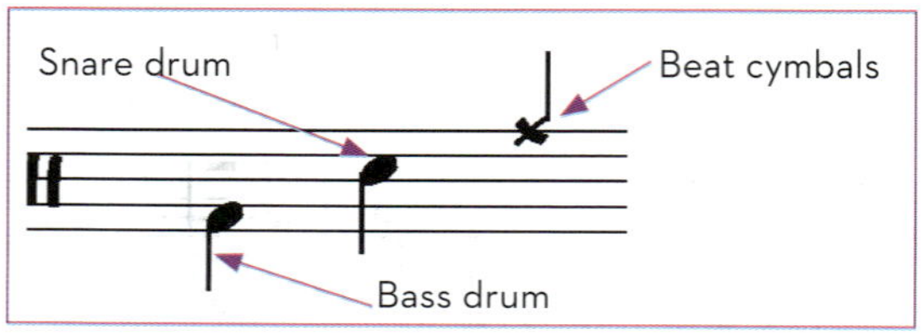

6 In Tune

A. Train Your Voice

Your voice should increase in range, but also in speed and flexibility. This exercise works on vocal agility. Sing it quickly, but be careful with your articulation and pronunciation of the syllables, exaggerating the consonants a little.

B. Reading Music

We will add a B note on the third line to those you already worked on. Mark a beat and say the names of the notes. You can do it many times with a faster beat in each repetition to become more fluent.

C. Repertoire

Now practice the intonation of the notes you worked on. Your teacher will show you how to sing this traditional African canon. You can sing it first with the names of the notes to practise reading the music, and then with the lyrics.

Banaha

(canon in three)

Traditional Congolese

> **WORKSHEET**
>
> 18. If you want to train your voice and sing with your friends better, remember the page useful expressions in regard to singing.

7 Move Your Fingers

WORKSHEET

19. See the glossary: useful expressions in regard to playing the recorder.

In this unit we will revise what you learnt in previous units and complicate some exercises a little.

In the accompaniments we use for the exercises, we can distinguish the following timbres:

- Accompaniment for *exercises 1, 2* and *3: drum set, bass guitar, synthesiser* and *ney.*
- Accompaniment for *exercises 4, 5* and *6: vocals, piano* and *English horn* (Figure 5.36).

Play the following exercises with your teacher's instructions.

Exercise 1

Exercise 2

Exercise 3

Exercise 4

Exercise 5

Exercise 6

Figure 5.36.
English horn: This instrument is from the oboe family, but its sound is lower.

8 Concert

Now we will play a nice piece called *Don D'Jembé*. This composition mainly uses instruments from the African continent: the *djembe* (Figure 5.37), *xylophone* (Figure 5.38) and *shekere*.

Don D'Jembé

Music: José Luis Salas

Figure 5.37.
Djembe.

Figure 5.38.
African xylophone or balafon.

Now we will use class instruments: keyboard percussion and recorders. This time we will not have recorded accompaniments: we will work independently and cooperatively to play *La pequeña tristeza* together.

La pequeña tristeza

Music: José Luis Salas

Download and print the worksheet you will find in the OLC to complete the concept map of the unit.

Musical instruments

Classified as

- **Families**
  - St……
    - B…… string — *Violin, viola, cello, double bass*
    - P…… string — *Harp, guitar*
    - S…… string — *Piano*
  - W……
    - W…… wind
      - Fl…… — *Transverse flute*
      - S…… reed — *Clarinet, saxophone*
      - D…… reed — *Oboe, bassoon*
    - B…… — *Trumpet, French horn, trombone, tuba*
  - P……
    - P…… — *Timpani, metallophone, glockenspiel, xylophone, bells*
    - Un…… — *Snare drum, bass drum, cymbals, triangle, bongos, castanets*
- **Musical ensembles**
  - O…… — Very large ensemble with string, woodwind, brass and percussion instruments
  - Ch…… music — Smaller ensembles: *duets, trios, quartets, chamber orchestra.* **String quartet:** *two violins, viola and cello*
  - B…… — Wind and percussion instruments
  - R…… band — *Electric guitar, bass guitar, drum set* (others: *keyboards*)
- **Other instruments**
  - Sch…… — *Glockenspiels, xylophones, metallophones, claves, wood block, guiro*
  - Instruments of the w…… — *Sitar, alphorn, quena, gamelan, steel drums, shamisen*

FINAL ACTIVITIES

1. **Classify the following instruments: *violin, piano, harp, double bass, guitar* and *cello.***
   - Bowed string
   - Plucked string
   - Struck string
2. **Do the following activities.**

   Classify the following instruments in the correct column: *saxophone, French horn, oboe, tuba, transverse flute, trumpet, bassoon, trombone* and *clarinet.*

Woodwind			Brass
Flutes	Single-reed	Double-reed	
...	...	...	...

3. **Place each percussion instrument into the correct column: *timpani, claves, snare drum, triangle, xylophone, bass drum, glockenspiel, maracas, bongos, metallophone* and *castanets.***

Pitched percussion	Unpitched percussion
...	...

4. **Put the following instruments in order from the highest-pitched to the lowest-pitched:**

   a) *Viola, double bass, cello* and *violin.*

   b) *Tuba, trumpet, trombone* and *French horn.*
5. **Answer the following questions:**

   a) Why is the orchestra conductor necessary?

   b) Indicate which are names of orchestra conductors: **Cristofori, Herbert von Karajan, Leonard Bernstein** and **Carl Orff.**
6. **Answer the following questions on instrumental ensembles:**

   a) What difference is there between a *symphony orchestra* and a *band*?

   b) What instruments are in a *string quartet*? And in a *rock band*?

7. Copy the following diagram of the placement of instruments in the orchestra in your Workbook and colour it according to the key:

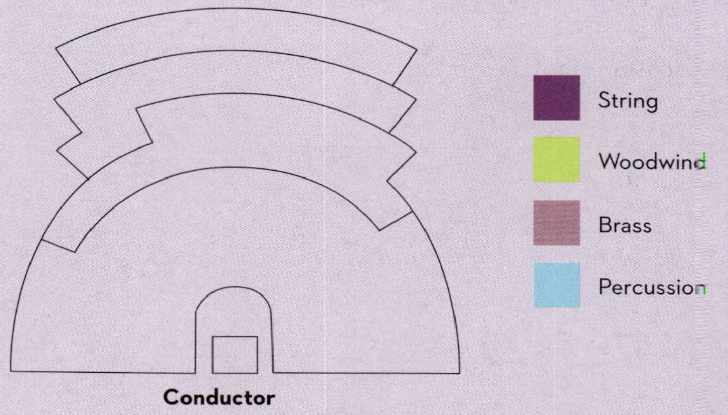

8. Write the names of these instruments in your Workbook.

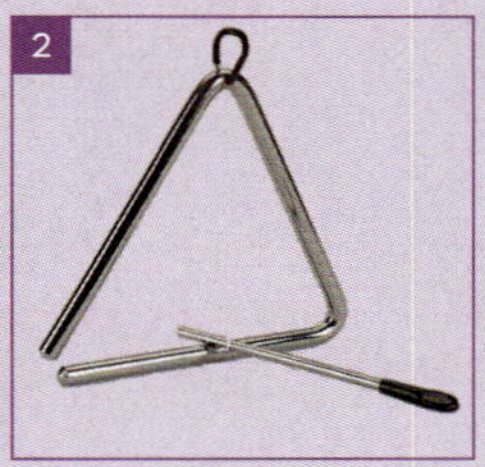

FINAL PROJECT

1. Form groups of 3 or 4 people to make an instrument together.
2. Watch the videos showing how to make home-made instruments.
3. Choose one instrument you like. Speak in English to decide which instrument you want to make together. Give your instrument a special name.
4. Prepare the materials and make your instrument. Bring it to the music room.
5. All the groups will show the instruments to the other classmates and explain how the instruments are made.
6. We will make an assessment report by filling in the OLC chart.

6 MUSICAL TEXTURE

Do you know what texture is? If you look in the *Oxford Advanced Learner's Dictionary*, you will find the following definition: 'the way a surface, substance or piece of cloth feels when you touch it'. So the textures of a wool sweater, a cotton shirt and a silk skirt are not the same. They give us different sensations.

But what does texture mean in music? Like a piece of cloth has different threads, there are different melodic lines in music. We have different types of musical texture depending on the combination of these melodic lines.

In this unit we will study what texture is in detail and we will analyse the main types of texture.

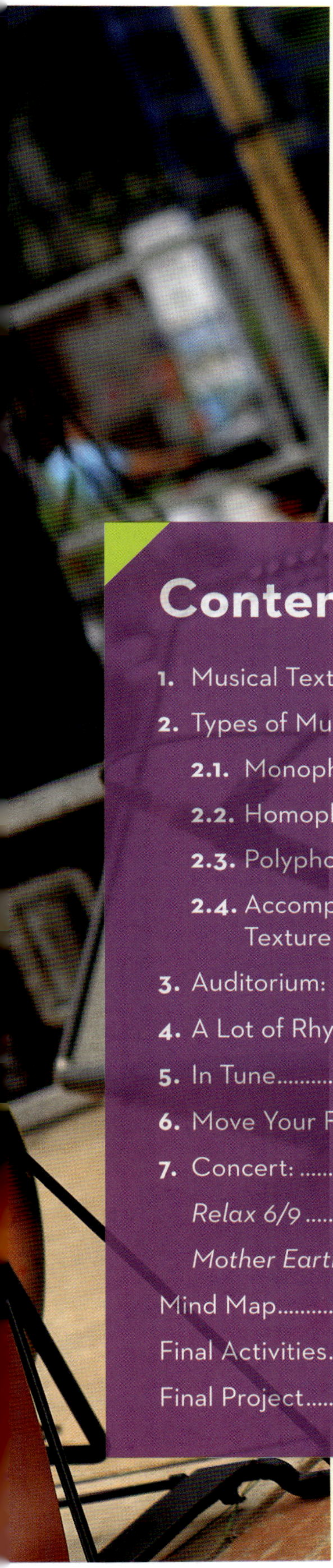

Contents

WORK ON THE TEXT

Download the worksheet 'Work on the text' and scan the text, or listen to your teacher, and write the keywords you read or hear from the introduction text.

1. T ... .
2. M ... line.
3. Musical t ... .

WARM UP

Download and watch some videos on YouTube about **'graphic scores'** and try to choose your favourite one.

1. What do you think is the simplest or the most complex music?
2. Do you think there is one important melody in every excerpt?
3. Did you know any excerpt?
4. Have you ever heard about the composers of these works?

FIND A CLASSMATE

Download and print the worksheet 'Which video do you prefer and why'?

- I prefer video ... composed by ... because ... .

1. Go around the class, ask your classmates and find a partner who likes or dislikes the same video as you.
2. Every pair must explain to the class their favourite videos and why they like them.

- We like video ... composed by ... because ... .

KEYWORDS

Download and print the activities that will guide you through the essential vocabulary of this unit.

1 Musical Texture

As we commented in the introduction to the unit, if we observe the world around us, we can find many types of textures (in clothes, in painting and even in food), which give us different sensations: the smoothness of silk, the roughness of a tree trunk and the coarseness of sandpaper.

For example, imagine an article of clothing: the fabric has different threads that come together in a certain way.

Something very similar occurs in music. The different elements (melodies, chords, etc.) can combine in different ways. Depending on how it is organised, we can have different results: the sound can be lighter or it can be much denser and richer.

Figure 6.1.
We can find very diverse textures around us.

We can define **musical texture** as the way we combine sounds in a musical composition.

Before studying the explanation of each one of the types of musical texture, we will do some practical exercises to experiment with different textures.

WORKSHEET

1. Download, read in class and fill in the gaps.
2. Download and complete the chart.
3. Visit Noteflight, listen and complete the activities.

ACTIVITIES

1. **Texture 1**

Think of your favourite food: it has a characteristic flavour, smell and texture. These come from the combination of different ingredients. But suppose that we start by using only one ingredient for this food, without mixing. It has a unique flavour. In music, this 'ingredient' is a melody like this one:

Do you know this melody? It is the famous French song *Frère Jacques* (known in English as *Brother John*). As it does not have any indications, one or many musicians can sing or play it at the same time.

- **Play the melody together with your classmates.**

As you have observed, it is one melody by itself, with nothing to accompany it.

This type of musical texture is called **monophonic** or **monodic texture.**

WORKSHEET

4. Put the words in the right order to make a definition of musical texture:

sounds / we combine / in a musical composition / the way.

ACTIVITIES

2. Texture 2

We continue developing our 'musical recipe' and combining more ingredients. Observe:

The lower melodic line (in green) is the original melody. We added a second melody (in pink). It moves with the same rhythm, but at a different pitch.

This musical texture is **homophonic texture.**

- **Play the previous example. (You can divide the class in two groups and each one plays a melody.)**

What do you feel in comparison with texture 1?

WORKSHEET

5. Visit Noteflight, listen and complete the activities.

3. Texture 3

Now we will combine the 'ingredients' in a different way. Observe carefully:

Can you explain what occurs in the bars in the purple box? If you notice, the upper line is the same melody as the lower one, but it starts two bars later. This means that the melodic lines do not coincide.

So the musical effect is two different melodies played at the same time. This makes it more difficult to follow the music.

This type of sound combination or texture, with several different melodies, is **polyphonic, counterpoint** or **contrapuntal texture.**

- **Divide the class in two groups and play the previous example.**

WORKSHEET

6. Visit Noteflight, listen and complete the activities.

ACTIVITIES

4. **Texture 4**

   Finally, we will look at a very familiar type of texture to you, because it represents most of your favourite musicians or bands: there is one soloist singer (*main melody*) and the rest of the musicians provide the *accompaniment*.

   Observe the example: we added a simple harmonic accompaniment to the melody of *Frère Jacques*.

This type of texture consists of a main melody (in green) with a harmonic accompaniment (in pink) and it receives the name **accompanied melody.**

- **Play the previous example: some of you play the accompaniment with keyboard and percussion instruments and the rest play the main melody.**

WORKSHEET

7. Visit Noteflight, listen and complete the activities.

ACTIVITIES

5. **Listen to the different types of texture that you played.**

A musical composition can alternate several of the textures we saw. Next we will analyse all these types of textures in detail.

Figure 6.2.
Music band El Canto del Loco. Much of the music you normally hear has an accompanied melody texture.

2 Types of Musical Texture

As we explained, depending on how the sounds combine in a composition, we can differentiate distinct types of texture. Here is a small summary:

Monophonic texture	one melodic line
Homophonic texture	several melodies with the same rhythm
Polyphonic texture	several independent or imitating melodies
Accompanied texture	main melody with a harmonic accompaniment

2.1. Monophonic Texture

Monophonic texture consists of only one melodic line, performed by one or several voices or instruments at the same time.

When several musicians perform the same melody simultaneously, they are singing or playing in *unison*. Example: Gregorian chant *(Kyrie)*.

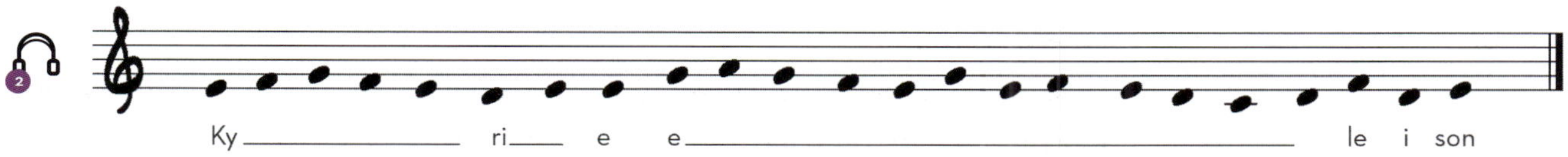

If you join all the notes with a line, you will have something similar to the following diagram: a melody with no type of accompaniment:

As you observed, the monodic or monophonic texture is the simplest, but it still has a certain magic. It was most common during most of the Middle Ages; in religious music, with the Gregorian chant; and in secular music, with the troubadours' songs.

Its use is also frequent in the traditional music of some cultures. Note that this type of texture facilitates the comprehension of the lyrics.

ACTIVITIES

6. **Try to sing the melody of the previous example with your classmates. You will observe that it has no rhythmic figures, because Gregorian chants have a very free rhythm marked by the phrases of the text.**

   Follow your teacher's indications to sing it simultaneously.

RESOURCES WEB

If you want to learn to listen to and sing Gregorian chants, check the website.

Link to the website:

http://www.abadiadesilos.es

WORKSHEET

8. As you read or listen to your teacher, download and complete the glossary.
9. Listen to the different excerpts throughout the unit, download and complete the chart.
10. Put the words in the right order to make a definition of monophonic texture:

    at the same time / performed / only one melodic line / by one or several voices.

2.2. Homophonic Texture

A composition has a **homophonic texture** when it has several melodies with different pitches, but the same rhythm.

Example: *Hallelujah* from the oratorio *Messiah*, by **Handel.**

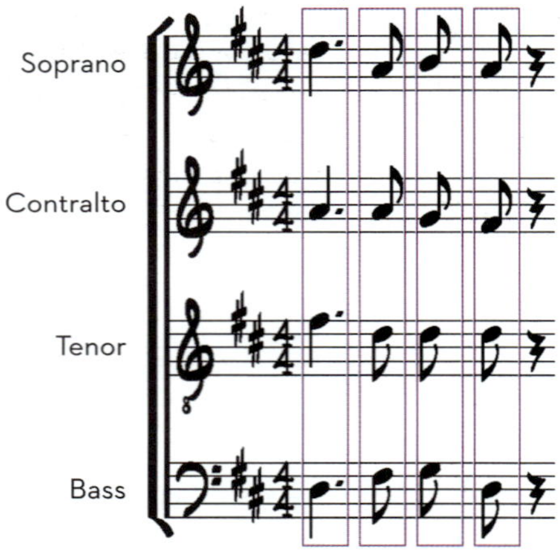

If you draw lines horizontally and vertically to join all the notes of the composition, you will have a diagram like the one below:

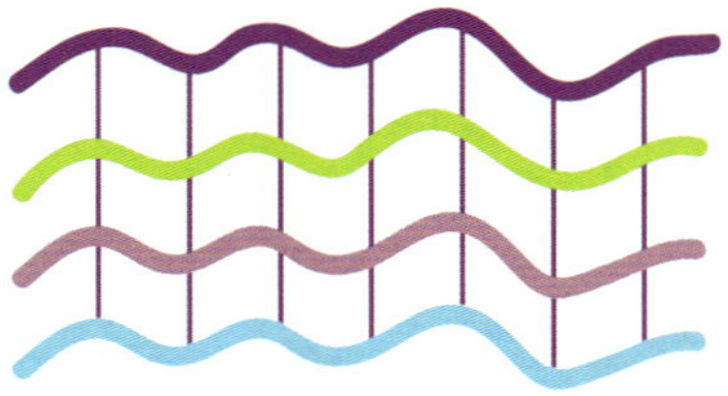

Several melodies with the same rhythm

On the left you can see bar 1 of the example above. The boxes indicate that the four voices move with the same rhythm, but each box has four different pitches.

WORKSHEET

11. Put the words in the right order to make a definition of homophonic texture:

    but the same rhythm / with different pitches / several melodies / A composition that has.

ACTIVITIES

7. Listen to the following recording with three musical excerpts. The styles are very different (rock, baroque and gospel), but note that in all three the voices sing in a homophonic texture. The excerpts are from the following compositions:

Bohemian Rhapsody (**Queen**)

Hallelujah (*Messiah*, by **Handel**)

If We Ever (**Take 6**)

2.3. Polyphonic Texture

Polyphonic texture is the superposition of various melodies that are independent or imitate each other.

We can compare this texture with a conversation between two or more people. One starts giving his/her opinion, and before he/she finishes, the other people begin to give theirs. As the two or more planes of conversation do not coincide, it is more difficult to follow them and understand what they are saying.

This is the densest texture that we have studied. It requires more effort from the listener to distinguish the different melodies that sound at the same time. Polyphony began at the end of the 11th century and was most popular in the Renaissance.

We also find examples of polyphony in Classicism, like the *Kyrie* of the *Requiem* by **Mozart.**

We can illustrate the polyphonic texture with this diagram:

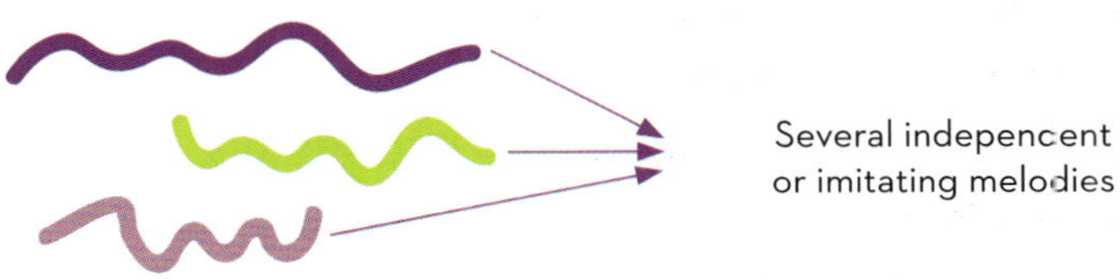

WORKSHEET

12. The strictest example of voices imitating each other is the **canon**. Various voices sound at the same time, performing the same melody but starting at different times.

    Search for a canon on YouTube and answer the questions.

13. Put in the right order the words to make a definition of Polyphonic texture:

    a superposition / or imitate each other / that are independent / of various melodies / A composition that has.

2.4. Accompanied Melody Texture

Accompanied melody texture is a main melody with a harmonic accompaniment.

We find an example of this type of music in classical music, where classical concerts with a soloist accompanied by the orchestra are very typical. So the melody is the star, and stands out over the accompaniment that enriches and complements it.

Example: *Piano Sonata No. 11, Op. 2* by Beethoven.

WORKSHEET

14. Put the words in the right order to make a definition of accompanied melody texture:

accompaniment / with a / harmonic / a main melody.

Piano Sonata No. 11, Op. 2

L. VAN BEETHOVEN

We can represent *accompanied melody* with this diagram:

WORKSHEET

15. Download and recapping:
    a) Work in groups of 3 or 6 and do activities 1, 2 and 3.
    b) True or false dictation.

This type of texture originated in the Baroque and played an important role in the birth of the opera, at the beginning of the 17th century. Its objective was to emphasise the main melody so it could be easier to understand the text.

Some composers of Classicism (second half of the 18th century) and Romanticism (19th century) used it a lot, too. It is also present in most contemporary music (pop, rock, etc.). You can play with the 'Follow on' Cards if you download them from the OLC.

Figure 6.3.
Stéphane Grappelli, one of the greatest jazz violinists of the 20th century.

ACTIVITIES

8. As you can see, accompanied melody texture is used in classical music and in contemporary music. Listen to the following examples and say who performs the main melody and who performs the accompaniment.

- *Lied* (*song*, in German) from the 19th century, by **Franz Schubert**
- *Djangology*, by **Stéphane Grappelli** (Figure 6.3)

3 Auditorium: *New Age* Music

A. The Facts

It is complicated to define *New Age* music because there are a large variety of styles. But we can try to define it as contemporary music that is generally melodic. It is evocative and its intention is to transmit different emotions and ideals: peace, relaxation, respect for our planet, etc.

The variety of styles include: *electronic, ethnic, folk, vocal, pop, jazz, classical,* etc. This mix of styles is the answer to a deep desire: to find new musical horizons, and definitively, 'new music'. We also use this description to refer to the *New Age* movement.

RESOURCES WEB

You will find a selection of *New Age* music excerpts on the website.

B. The Music

You will hear three musical excerpts from the following *New Age* musicians:

- The first is from the American saxophonist **Paul Winter** (Figure 6.4) and his group the **Paul Winter Consort.** It was one of the most representative groups of *New Age* music during the eighties and nineties. This group mixes its music with very diverse cultural elements: ethnic music, jazz, sounds of nature, etc. They won three Grammy awards and received eight nominations. Listen to an excerpt from the song *Ocean Dream*, in which the song of whales combines with Paul's soprano saxophone and the rest of the ensemble.
- The second excerpt is from the Irish group **Nightnoise.** They were also pioneers of new music during the eighties and nineties. Their compositions are full of Celtic music mixed with classical music. Some experts call this *chamber-folk* music. The title of the song you will hear is *Shuan*.
- The last recording is by **Enya** (Figure 6.5). She is a singer and pianist who was born in Ireland in 1961. She is one of the most famous *New Age* singers, but she does not like to consider her music part of this genre.

  Her album *Watermark*, which came out at the end of 1988, was at the top of British rankings in its first week. Currently, she has sold six and a half million copies around the world. Now you will hear an excerpt from the song *Orinoco Flow*.

Figure 6.4.
Paul Winter

Figure 6.5.
Enya, one of the most representative singers of *New Age* music

WORKSHEET

16. Listen to the excerpts and make your ideal **list of musical hits.**
17. Read or listen to your teacher and complete the **glossary.**

4 A Lot of Rhythm

WORKSHEET

18. See the glossary: useful expressions in regard to rhythm.

In this unit we will work on the rhythmic formula *off-beat quaver*.

The formula consists of substituting the first quaver for a rest. We used the syllables *ti-ti* for studying quavers. Now you can substitute the first *ti* for the syllable *one* like this:

As the syllable *one* represents a rest, you do not play when you say it.

Do the following rhythm exercises by clapping your hands or tapping your knees, alternating hands. You can also use rhythm syllables. Then do them with the recording.

Exercise 1

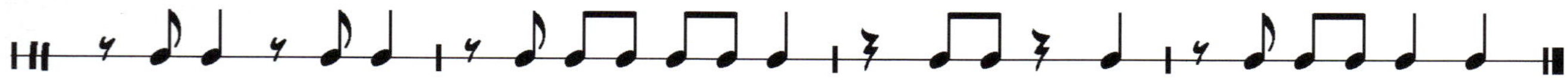

Exercise 2

Practise these polyrhythms with two hands on your knees. You can also do them with *bongos:*

Exercise 3

Practise the following drum patterns with body percussion. Then play them with the recording.

Exercise 4

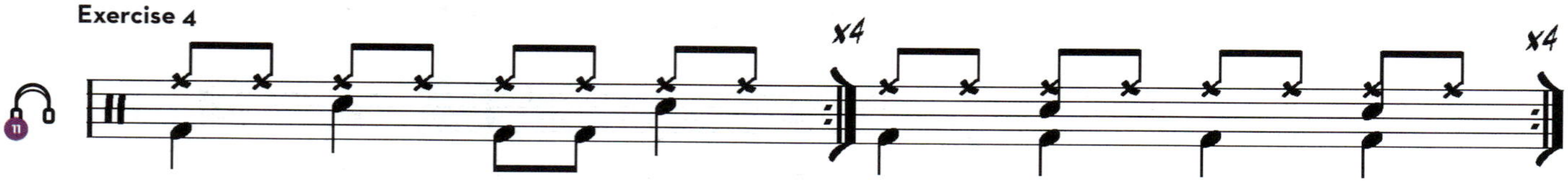

5 In Tune

A. Train Your Voice

In this exercise you will sing the same music phrase first in a minor key and then in a major key. Be careful with the tuning of the notes. The harmonic accompaniment in the unit resources will help you.

DID YOU KNOW?

There are people who have absolute pitch (or perfect pitch). They recognise notes when they hear them.

B. Reading Music

We will add a C note on the third space to those you already worked on.

WORKSHEET

19. If you want to train your voice and sing better with your friends, remember the page useful expressions in regard to singing.

C. Repertoire

Sing this melody. The harmony is based on a famous canon by the composer Pachelbel. Sing it first with notes to practise reading music, and then with the lyrics. When you have learnt it well, you can try to sing it in a canon with your classmates (in 2, 3 or 4 voices).

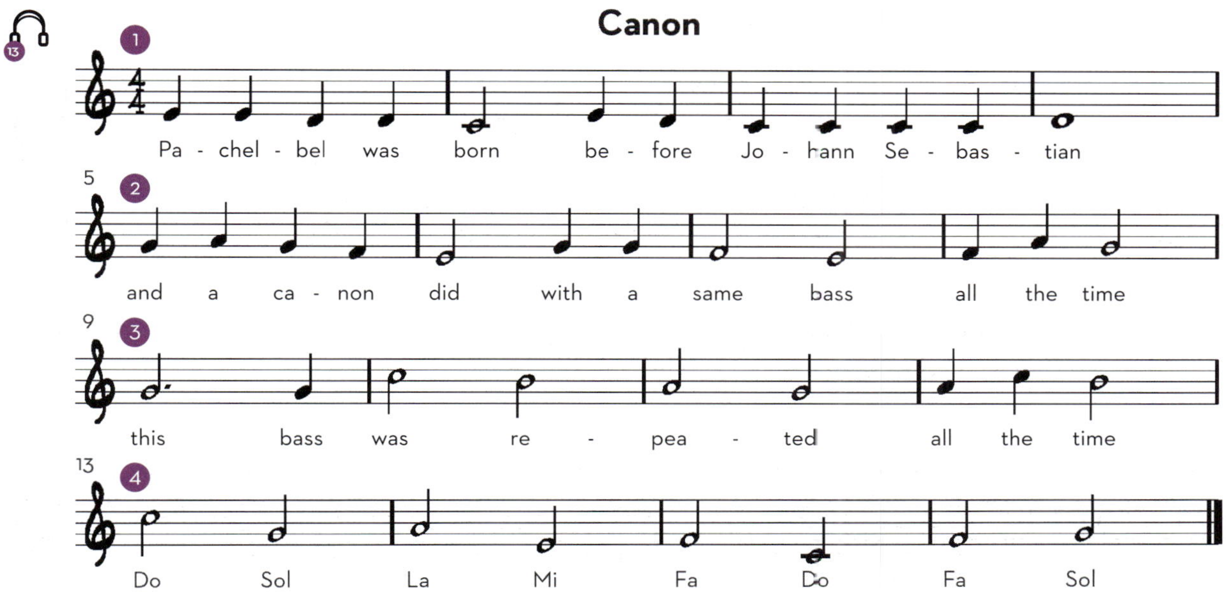

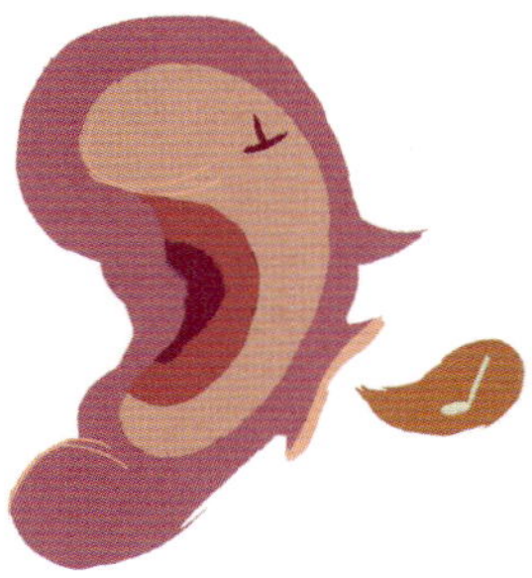

Figure 6.6.
The didgeridoo is a wind instrument used by the Australian Aborigines.

6 Move Your Fingers

We continue practising the notes learnt in previous units.

The background music we will use in this unit is the following:

- Accompaniment for *exercises 1, 2* and *3*: rock background music with the *Hammond organ* and other instruments.
- Accompaniment for *exercises 4, 5* and *6*: this music makes us imagine a jungle. We will hear a curious instrument: *the didgeridoo* (Figure 6.6).

Play the following exercises with your teacher's instructions. Remember that you can use the accompaniments included on the unit resources at home and in class to make the practice more interesting.

Exercise 1

Exercise 2

Exercise 3

Exercise 4

Exercise 5

Exercise 6

7 Concert

This piece's title, *Relax 6/9*, is because of two very important elements. First, the word *relax* defines the character of the piece (relaxed, ambient), as it refers to a type of music characterised by its tranquil melodies, ambient sounds, etc. Secondly, *6/9* refers to the use of chords in these intervals (6th and 9th). This gives the song a very characteristic sound.

This musical trend, as we saw in the *Auditorium* section of this unit, is called *New Age* music.

Figure 6.7.
Suzanne Ciani (composer, pianist and pioneer in the area of electronic music) is one of the first women to become known in the world of *New Age* music. She received five Grammy award nominations and one Golden Globe award.

Relax 6/9

Mother Earth is the next piece we will play with the recorder. It is a rhythmic, emotional composition which includes various musical styles: ethnic and symphonic OST. This piece wants to transmit a message of hope for the conservation of our planet. You can hear ethnic instruments like the didgeridoo and the song of whales.

Mother Earth

Music: José Luis Salas

Download and print the worksheet you will find in the OLC to complete the concept map of the unit.

Musical texture

This is the w ... of c ... different s ... in a musical c ... .

Types of musical texture

M ... phonic Only o ... melodic l ..., performed by one or m ... voices or i ... at the s ... t ... .

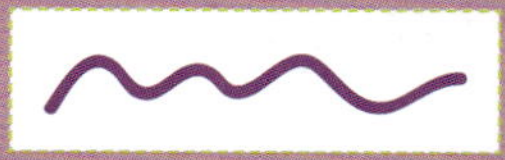

H ... p ... c V ... melodies with different p ... but the same r ... .

P ... V ... melodies move i ... or i ... each other.

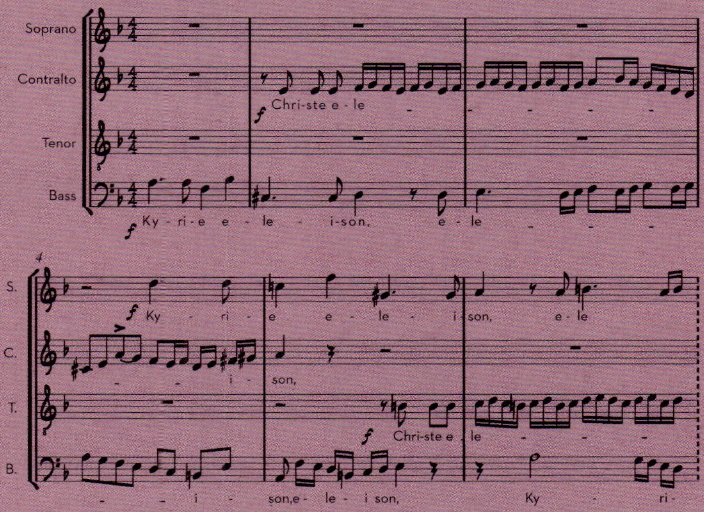

A ... melody A m ... melody with a h ... a ... .

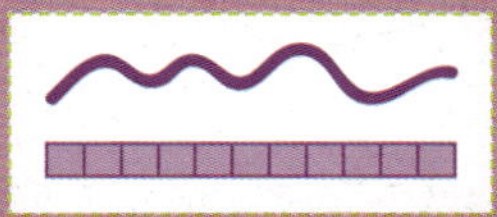

1. Look at the following examples and decide what texture they have:

a) Confiteor (Credo for the Mass in B Minor BWV 232), by **J.S. Bach**

b) Cantiga (Song), by **Alfonso X el Sabio (the Wise)**

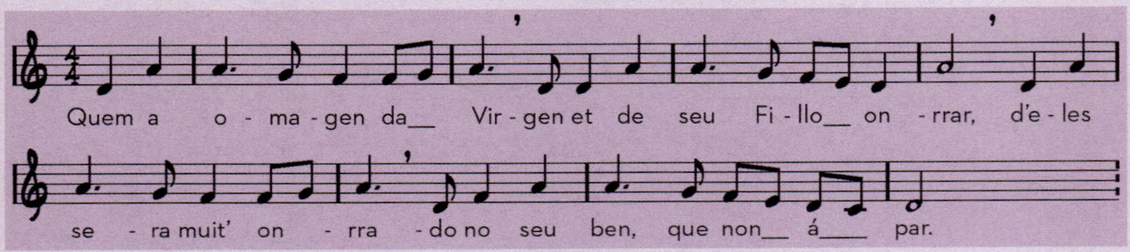

c) Christmas carol *Ay triste que vengo* by **Juan del Encina**

d) Lied 'Standchen' (serenade) *of Schwanengesang*, by **Franz Schubert**

2. Compose a canon in three voices. The main melody is already written in the exercise. Write the other two voices in your Workbook.

Canon in Three Voices

FINAL PROJECT

In groups of 4 or 5.

1. Choose 2 o 3 different excerpts of music you like. Try to choose very different kinds of music, different styles or different textures.

2. Make a research worksheet about the composer of the work you have chosen (work, style, life story, biography, etc.).

3. Try to represent the textures graphically with lines, shapes, rows or figures, comparing all the excerpts in different posters or in the same poster.

4. You can make a collage on posterboard or a digital poster with the shapes and rows of your writing program (Paint) or in an online application you find on the web.

5. Show the picture to your classmates and follow the graphic while you are listening to the excerpt of music.

6. Compare your classmates' graphics and try to assess every project with your teacher's help.

   You can discuss with your classmates what you liked about each presentation and suggest ways to improve them.

7 MUSICAL FORM

In other units, you studied the different elements that the composer uses to create a piece of music (melody, harmony, rhythm, texture, timbre, etc.). You saw that the possibilities are infinite. The composer has to organise his/her musical ideas and 'shape' them to transmit what he/she wants to express.

In plastic arts (like architecture, sculpture or painting) something similar happens. The artist must plan how to organise the different elements in the space to create a structure.

In music, this develops over time, so we will have to use our memory to understand this internal organisation. This differentiates music, a temporal art (like cinema and theatre), from plastic arts. In this unit we will give you the keys to understand the structure of musical compositions.

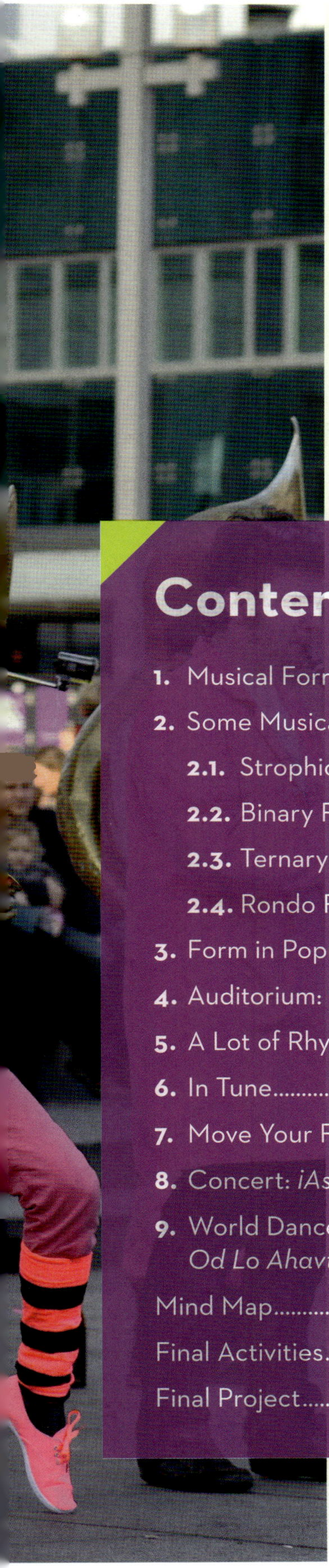

Contents

WORK ON THE TEXT

Download the worksheet 'Work on the text', read page 116 and fill in the gaps in the activity.

WARM UP

Download and answer the questions.

1. Scan the chapter headings, pictures and graphics in the unit (pages 118-124) and write the keywords in the diagram.
2. Watch a video about 'MUSICAL FORM' (or a similar one on YouTube) and write 4 sentences that summarise it.

FIND A CLASSMATE

1. Compare with your classmate and add:
   a) more sentences to warm up activity 2.
   b) more words to the keywords diagram.
2. Do the same in groups of 4 and finally share the information with your teacher on the blackboard.

KEYWORDS

1. After doing warm up activity 1 fill in the OLC keywords diagram.
2. While you work on Unit 7 make a glossary of musical and not so musical terms that you do not understand. You have some clues in the OLC.

1 Musical Form

Every artistic composition has a structure, whether it is a work of architecture, a sculpture or a book.

For example, look at the following dialogue:

- *But everyone said it would be fun.*
- *It was very boring.*
- *How was Luis' party last night?*
- *Well, no, it was terrible.*

The sentences are not in a logical order, so the dialogue does not make sense. We need to 'shape' it.

Figure 7.1.

It is important to know the difference between form and style. Look at the picture above. It is a painting by **Velázquez**. Which modern artist painted the same painting with the same structure but with a completely different style? If you need help, you can find more information on the website about *cubism*, one of the first artistic vanguards.

ACTIVITIES

1. Organise the sentences of the text above so that it makes sense.

As we explained in the unit introduction, music also needs a **form** or structure. You ask how a composer organises his/her **musical ideas** so they are logical and coherent. Do the following activity to understand this better.

ACTIVITIES

2. Here are some different musical ideas:

Perform the melodies above on the recorder or a keyboard percussion instrument, following the order indicated by the colours. We suggest various possibilities:

Performance 1

Performance 2

Performance 3

WORKSHEET

1. Download and fill in the gaps.
2. Download and write a synonym for 'musical form'.

In the previous activity, we did three different performances by selecting and organising the musical ideas in different ways.

Musical form is the way we organise musical ideas in a musical composition (its *structure*).

In music, this structure or form is represented by the letters of the alphabet: A, B, C, etc. These name each part of a composition. But what criteria are there for using one letter or another? Very simple: the first musical idea is **A**, the second idea is **B**, the third is **C**, etc.

We can also repeat a theme with a modification. In this case, we use the same letter with the symbol ' (for example, a variation of **A** is **A'**, and we say it as *A prime*).

If you look at the musical ideas you played on the previous page, we can call them:

A

B

A'

ACTIVITIES

3. Which combination of letters can you use to name each of these compositions according to its parts?

From what we explained before, we can deduce the different types of **procedures** (principles or processes) that a composer follows to create a composition and determine its structure. They are: **repetition**, **contrast** and **variation.**

Imagine you are the composer. Think of a theme A. You can:

- Repeat it again. — A A **Repetition**
- Use a different theme that contrasts with the previous one. — A B **Contrast**
- Repeat it with a modification. — A A' **Variation**

WORKSHEET

3. Jumbled definition: download and fill in the diagram.
4. Answer the questions:
   a) What is the name in music for the first musical idea we hear in a musical composition?
   b) And for the second and third idea?
5. Download and do the activity about procedures by filling in the gaps.

DID YOU KNOW?

Minimalist music uses the repetition of sequences of notes or basic elements, with slightly different nuances, to create a hypnotic atmosphere. We also call it repetitive music. Its main composers include **Steve Reich** and **Philip Glass**. You can find more information about minimalism on the resources website.

WORKSHEET

6. Download and fill in the gaps.
7. Search for and watch a video about musical forms.

   What are the forms named in the video?

2 Some Musical Forms

In the history of music, composers have created a large variety of musical forms. Many of them have been models for later composers.

As we saw in the previous section, the combination of different musical ideas (**A**, **B**, **C**, etc.) can make different *forms*. We create these with the **principles** of repetition, contrast and variation. Next we will see some of them.

2.1. Strophic Form

You probably know the following children's song. Although the two verses have different lyrics, they repeat the same music.

This form has one musical section or phrase that repeats. We call it **strophic form**. As you can see, it uses repetition and it is common in many popular songs. We can represent it with this diagram:

A	A	...

2.2. Binary Form

We say that a musical composition has a **binary form** when it has two different musical **sections.** It uses contrast of different musical ideas (**A** and **B**). These sections can repeat, but the musical form does not vary. For example:

A B or AA BB

ACTIVITIES

4. **Listen to the following recording. It is from a piece from the Renaissance. It has a binary form A, B, and it repeats two times: the first time instruments are played and the second time is vocal.**

Instrumental part	Vocal part
A B	AA BB

You can see the two themes (A and B) of this recording in the score below.

Now is the Month of Maying

WORKSHEET

8. Download and answer true o false.

Are these letters the right types of forms?

1. A+A: Binary form
2. A+B: Strophic form
3. A+A: Binary form
4. AA+BB: Strophic form
5. A+A'+A'': Strophic form

DID YOU KNOW?

The introduction and the coda

We can find an *introduction* and a *coda* in many musical compositions.

The **introduction** is a musical fragment at the beginning of a piece to prepare the entrance of the main theme. The **coda** is a fragment added to the end of the piece to accentuate the feeling of ending.

WORKSHEET

9. Search for videos about ternary form on YouTube.
   Watch the videos and write the name of the composer and works you heard.
   Also answer the complementary questions about Mozart's famous variations in the OLC.

2.3. Ternary Form

This form is called ternary because it has three sections: the first and the second are contrasting, whereas the third is usually a repetition or variation of the first. It corresponds to the following diagram:

A B A or A B A'

Did you know that **Mozart** wrote *variations* for piano of the famous song *Twinkle, Twinkle, Little Star*? Here is the melody. Notice that it has a ternary form:

Twinkle, Twinkle, Little Star

REMEMBER

First and second endings

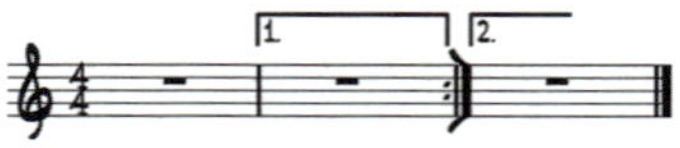

1st time

2nd time

When you do the second repetition, skip the 1st ending and play the 2nd ending.

***Da capo* (D.C.)**

This means 'from the beginning' and it indicates a complete repetition of the piece.

When it includes the indication *'al Fine'*, you must finish where *'Fine'* is written.

ACTIVITIES

5. Revise the **repeat signs** and play the following rhythm exercises. Before trying to play them, revise the meaning of each of the signs that appear.

2.4. Rondo Form

Imagine the following situation: a reporter walks along the street interviewing different people about their favourite places to go for the summer holiday.

Reporter: Excuse me, where is your favourite place to go for the summer holiday?

Woman: Well, I like the beach, because the sea water feels very nice.

Reporter: Excuse me, where is your favourite place to go for the summer holiday?

Business man: I like the mountains, because I can escape from the stress of daily life.

Reporter: Excuse me, where is your favourite place to go for the summer holiday?

Boys: We like to travel to see new cities.

You notice that this dialogue alternates between the reporter's question and the different answers. The question is always the same, but the answers are different:

Question	Answer 1	Question	Answer 2	Question	Answer 3

This diagram is very similar to the **rondo** form. A *chorus* or section **A** alternates with other different sections (**B**, **C**, **D**, etc.). But this musical form always finishes with theme A. So there is a balance between the repetition and the contrast.

A	B	A	C	A	D	...	A

ACTIVITIES

6. **Listen to the overture of the opera *Carmen*, by Bizet. It is a very clear example of rondo form (ABACA). Below are the beginnings of the three main themes of sections A, B and C.**
   a) Compare the three melodies (their melodic and rhythmic design, the nuances, etc.).
   b) Listen to the recording and indicate when each section begins.

WORKSHEET

10. Musical diagram:

    There are also other rondo forms like *Raider's March* by the composer John Williams in the film Indiana Jones.

    Fill in the musical diagram in the OLC.

3 Form in Popular Music

Figure 7.2.
Live performance by **La Oreja de Van Gogh.**

Maybe you think about the musical form of the songs you normally listen to. There is a series of **musical parts** that are usually combined in the songs of this style to shape them. Can you name some of these parts?

You can probably think of the words *verse* and *chorus*. These two parts are usually present in a song. But they are not the only parts we use, as you can see here:

Introduction	This **prepares** the musical atmosphere of the song at the **beginning.**
Verse	This **tells** the story or **plot** of the song. There are usually several verses, separated by the chorus.
Bridge	As its name indicates, this is a musical part that connects the verse and chorus. It is normally shorter than them.
Chorus	This part **expresses the general feeling** of the song. It appears several times in the song. We normally use it to finish the song by repeating several times. It is the catchiest and most attractive section of the song.
Solo	An **instrument** (usually the *electric guitar* or the *sax*) **improvises** a melody in this musical part.
Interlude	Any **instrumental part** that is not the introduction or the coda, and is **not improvised.**
Coda	This **final** part is the **conclusion** of the song.

Vocal parts **Instrumental parts**

WORKSHEET

11. Now that you have learnt a lot about form, make a mind map with all the keywords of the unit. See the glossary in the OLC.
12. Do the OLC activity 'Follow' on cards and in groups of 6.

ACTIVITIES

7. **Listen to the first part of the song *Atrapados en la red*, by the band Tam Tam Go. You can hear an intro, a verse, a bridge and a chorus. Follow this *music diagram* as you listen.**

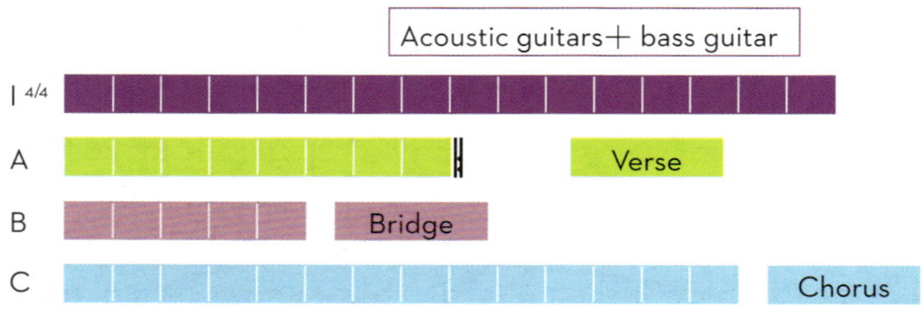

4 Auditorium: Latin American Music

A. The Facts

We normally use the term *Latin American music* and the word *salsa* as synonyms to define the mix of varied sounds and rhythms present in Latin America. In the sixties of the 20th century, *Beatlemania*, the *twist* and *rock and roll* fever seemed to cover up other artistic manifestations, but life gives you surprises (as Rubén Blades says in his song *Pedro Navaja*), and everything changed.

Mambo, cha-cha-cha, merengue, Cuban son, rumba, jazz fusion, etc.: There are many names and sometimes it is difficult to know the differences. **Izzy Sanabria** proposed the term salsa and this style became an international phenomenon.

B. The Music

Latin American music has certain common **characteristics:** an introduction, a melodic phase, a phase of rhythm or percussion called *montuno*, a phase of dialogues between the soloist and the backing vocalists and an ending. Instrumentally, as it is very syncopated and rhythmic, percussion instruments (*congas*, *pailas*, *guiros*, *claves*, etc.) and a wind section (*brass* and *saxes*) are essential.

Let's go through the music of some of the **most representative artists** of this genre.

In the decade of 1960, the percussionist and orchestra director **Tito Puente** and the singer **Celia Cruz** were the main representatives of the genre. Listen to **Celia Cruz** in her version of the famous cha-cha-cha *Oye como va*, by the guitarist **Carlos Santana.**

The album *Siembra* (1978), a collaboration between **Rubén Blades** (Figure 7.3) and **Willie Colón**, was the first to sell over a million copies only in the United States. One of the songs of this album, *Pedro Navaja*, had record sales and is considered to be one of the classics of salsa of all times.

In the decade of the eighties, the composer and singer **Juan Luis Guerra** (Figure 7.4) marked a different way of living, feeling and listening to merengue. He knows how to show the reality of a country through very poetic lyrics. His song *El Niágara en bicicleta* is a criticism of the difficulties and misery in some countries.

Gloria Estefan, one of the most important figures of Latin American music in the world, always says that her dream is to be able to sing in a free Cuba. When she was little she had to abandon the island (Cuba) because of the political situation of the country. We finish this auditorium session on Latin American music with her song *Cuba libre*.

Figure 7.3.
Rubén Blades.

Figure 7.4.
Juan Luis Guerra.

WORKSHEET

13. Answer the questions:
    a) What is salsa?
    b) Who proposed this name?
    c) Do you know the main genres in Latin music?

    Listen to the music and fill in the listening chart in the OLC.

RESOURCES WEB

You can find the lyrics to *Pedro Navaja*, *El Niágara en bicicleta* and *Cuba libre* on the website.

WORKSHEET

14. See the glossary: useful expressions in regard to rhythm.

5 A Lot of Rhythm

In this unit we will work on the rhythmic formula *syncopa:*

Do the following rhythm exercises by clapping your hands or tapping your knees, alternating hands. You can also use rhythm syllables. Then play them with the recording.

Exercise 1

Exercise 2

Exercise 3

Do the following exercise with body percussion.

Exercise 4

Practise the following drum patterns with body percussion. Then play them with the recording.

6 In Tune

A. Reading Music

We add the D note on the third line of the staff to those you already worked on.

WORKSHEET

15. See the glossary: useful expressions in regard to tuning your voice.

B. Repertoire

In this unit we will perform a *Negro spiritual* (Figure 7.5). This music style emerged in connection with African slaves. They had to go to plantations in the United States. The slaves sang these melodies for consolation and motivation to face their difficult situation.

The beauty of these songs made many musicians interested in them. They made evocative accompaniments and four-part arrangements. Many choirs sing them today around the world.

Sing the following spiritual with the recorded backing track. Sing it first with the names of the notes and when you know the melody well, sing it with the lyrics.

Figure 7.5.
There are a lot of **choirs specialised in spirituals** in the United States. In the rest of the world, an increasing number of choirs and artists include this music style in their repertoire.

Swing Low, Sweet Chariot

WORKSHEET

16. See the glossary: useful expressions in regard to playing the recorder.

7 Move Your Fingers

It is time to take another step in our learning.

- Accompaniment for *exercises 1, 2* and *3*: Background music made with Celtic instruments. We studied these in Unit 4: *tin whistles, bodhran* and *Celtic harp.*
- Accompaniment for exercises *4, 5* and *6*: We will travel to the Islamic world by listening to some of its traditional instruments: *lute* (Figure 7.6), *psaltery* and *darbuka* (Figure 7.7).

Exercise 1

Exercise 2

Exercise 3

Exercise 4

Exercise 5

Exercise 6

Figure 7.6.
Arabic lute: plucked string instrument.

Figure 7.7.
Darbuka: traditional percussion instrument from the Arabic culture.

8 Concert

The piece you will play in this Concert section is a tribute to the 'Queen of Salsa', **Celia Cruz** (Figure 7.8). In 1959, after the triumph of the Cuban Revolution, she had to abandon her country (Cuba). She continued her career abroad and became one of the most emblematic figures of Latin American music around the world. The title of the piece is from one of her most famous and fun expressions: *¡Asúcar!*.

The beauty of the piece fuses the rhythm of the *cha-cha-cha* with a characteristic sound of guitar distortion. This is a tribute to another great artist of Latin American music fused with blues, jazz and rock: the guitarist **Carlos Santana.**

Figure 7.8.
Celia Cruz.

¡Asúúúcar sabroso!

Music: José Palazón

9 World Dance Workshop

In this unit we will learn a **traditional dance from Israel**. Israeli folkloric dance emerged as a mix of Jewish and non-Jewish folkloric dances from many places of the world.

As the population has many diverse origins, the new people brought their native dances to the newly-created State of Israel and adapted them to the new environment. Among them, a Romanian dance, the *hora*, represented the new life that they were building in Israel. They dance in a ring. This means that all the participants are equals. The simple movements let everyone participate and their linked arms symbolise the new ideology.

The general enthusiasm for dance led to a multifaceted genre of folkloric dance. They based it on popular Israeli songs, but incorporated influences from the Arab tradition, such as the *debka* and dance elements from American jazz, Latin American rhythms and the typical cadences of Mediterranean countries.

We will learn the choreography based on the Israeli song *Od lo ahavtidai* (I Have Not Loved Enough Yet), by the composer Naomi Shemer. She wrote several very emblematic songs for the people of Israel.

DID YOU KNOW?

The Karmiel Dance Festival is celebrated every year and it is the largest dance celebration in Israel. It consists of three or four days and nights of continuous dancing, 5,000 dancers and a quarter of a million people in the audience.

RESOURCES WEB

You can find a video of this dance performed by secondary students and another with an explanation of how to perform it on the website.

WORKSHEET

17. See the glossary: useful expressions in regard to dancing.

Choreography Summary

The choreography you will learn for this dance begins with all the participants in a circular position (ring). It has two parts:

- **Part A:** The dancers turn sideways in a clockwise direction, alternating the side step called *mayim* with the forward step called *cherkessia*. They use these steps a lot in Israeli dances.
- **Part B:** They combine going in and out of the circle (while clapping) with jumping toward the right, and then going around the circle.

Download and print the worksheet you will find in the OLC to complete the concept map of the unit.

- **Musical f ...**
  - What is it? — The w ... we o ... musical i ... in a musical c ... .
  - How is it represented? — We r ... every different musical s ... or i ... with the l ... of the alphabet: **A**, **B**, **C.**
  - Compositional p ... — The procedures a composer f ... to cr ... a com ... determine the s ... They are:
    - **R** ...: A A
    - **C** ...: A B
    - **V** ...: A A'
- **Some musical forms**
  - S ... form — It is a r ... ing musical s ... or phrase: A A ...
  - B ... form — There are ... different musical s ... : A B
  - T ... form — It has ... sections. The first and the second are c ... ing, and the third is a r ... or v ... of the first: A B A or A B A'
  - R ... form — A ch ... (**A**) alternates with different v ... (**B**, **C**, **D** ...): A B A C A D ... A
- **F ... in pop music**
  - V ... parts
    - Verse — Tells the s ... of the song
    - Bridge — C ... the *verse* and the *chorus*
    - Chorus — Ex ... the general f ... of the song
  - I ... parts
    - Introduction — Beginning, p ... the atmosphere
    - Solo — Im ... of a soloist instrument
    - Interlude — Ins ... part without im ...
    - Coda — End, c ... of the song

FINAL ACTIVITIES

1. **What is the *musical form*? Try to explain it in your own words.**

2. **Practise the procedures of *repetition*, *contrast* and *variation*. With the following sentences think of three others with the indications:**

   I like to play the recorder because it is fun.

   Repetition: (...)   Contrast: (...)   Variation: (...)

3. **We will do something similar to the previous exercise but using rhythms instead of sentences:**

   a) Use the example rhythm (**A**) and make a different rhythm, (**B**) (contrast) and another that is a variation of the first (**A'**).

   Example rhythm (**A**):

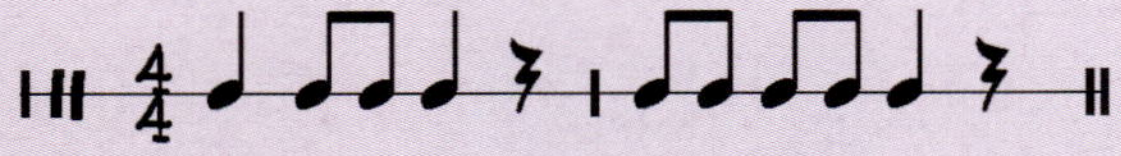

   b) Next, join them to create rhythm compositions with different forms.

   For example:

   AA   **AA'**   **AABB**   **ABA**   **ABA'**

   c) Finally, play your composition in class.

4. **Match each of the following diagrams with the musical form in your Workbook:**

Strophic form	A B
Binary form	A B A'
Ternary form	A A A ...
Rondo form	A B A C A D ... A

5. **Find the piece of music *Pangea* (*Concert* section of Unit 1) in your book. Write its form using the letters of the alphabet, as you learnt in this unit. Does its structure coincide with one of the types of musical forms that appear in the previous activity?**

6. **You performed *Hip Night Hop* in Unit 3. Analyse it and answer the following questions in your Workbook:**

   a) Which bars make the verse? And the chorus?

   b) Do you think the piece has a bridge? Why?

   c) Do you think the four bars of scratching in the middle are a *solo* or an *interlude*?

7. **Write the correct answer to the following questions in your Workbook:**

- *Da Capo* is:

  a) A repeat sign.

  b) A prolongation sign.

  c) A character indication.

- What is the name of the musical fragment placed at the end of a piece to give it more feeling of conclusion?

  a) Extension.

  b) Coda.

  c) Close.

- We call a musical fragment that precedes a piece to prepare the entrance of the main theme the:

  a) Preamble.

  b) Presentation.

  c) Introduction.

8. **In your Workbook, practise writing music and copy the following examples without using repeat signs:**

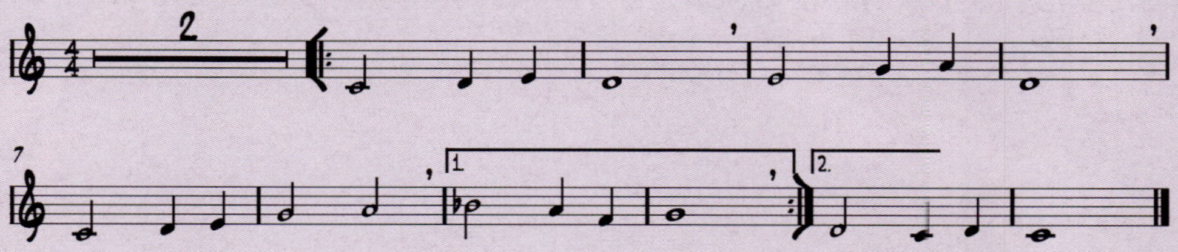

FINAL PROJECT

1. Make groups of 4 or 5 people.
2. You are going to create two compositions: a rhythmic one and a melodic one with a specific structure. The first one has a free structure. The second one is in rondo form.
3. You will have to write or represent your musical compositions graphically.
4. Perform them with body percussion, voice or instruments. Start with the rhythmic composition and when you finish start with the melodic one.
5. Write or represent the compositions on paper or in Noteflight (online app).
6. Perform them for the class.
7. Assess the other groups' compositions.

8 POPULAR URBAN MUSIC

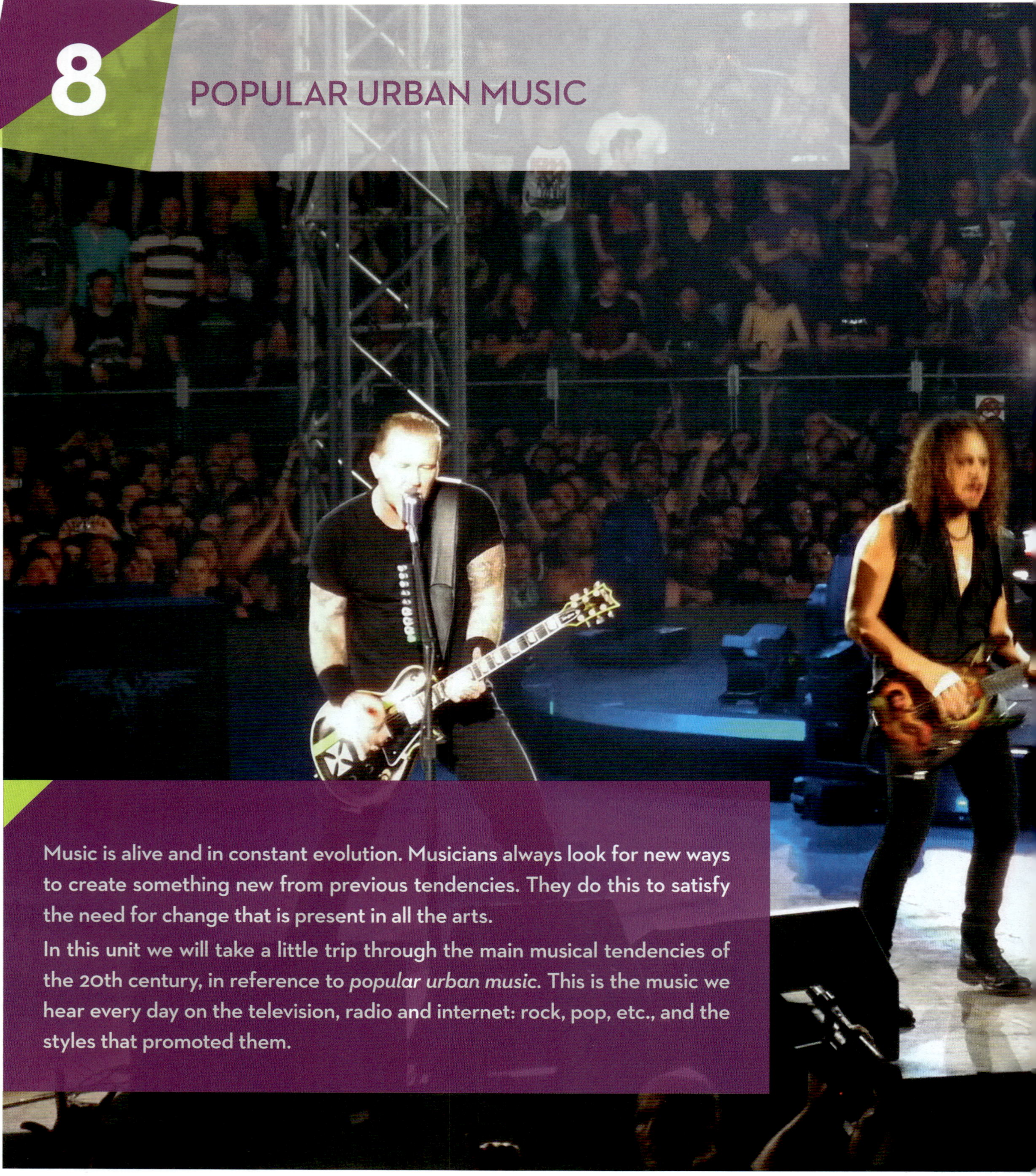

Music is alive and in constant evolution. Musicians always look for new ways to create something new from previous tendencies. They do this to satisfy the need for change that is present in all the arts.

In this unit we will take a little trip through the main musical tendencies of the 20th century, in reference to *popular urban music*. This is the music we hear every day on the television, radio and internet: rock, pop, etc., and the styles that promoted them.

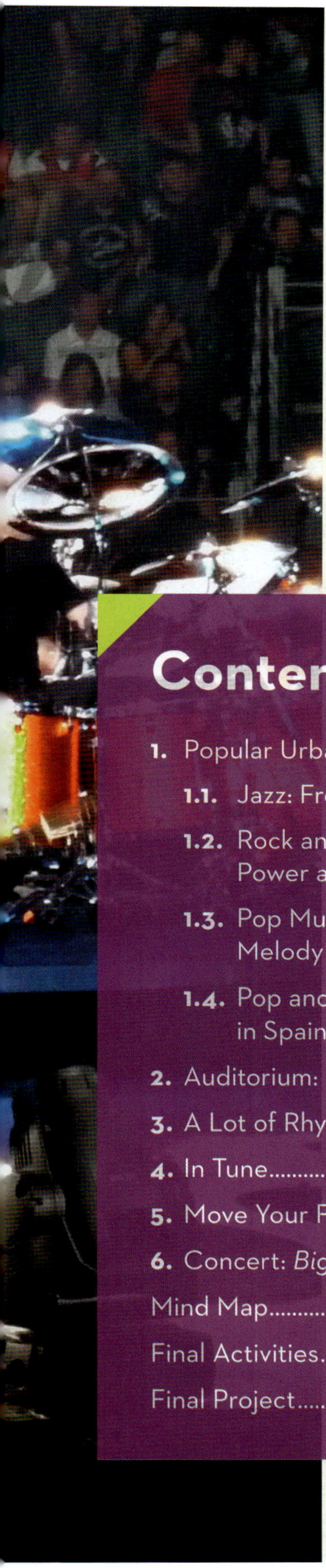

Contents

WORK ON THE TEXT

Read with your teacher, download the worksheet and fill in the gaps.

WARM UP

1. Things I know and like about... Popular urban music.
   a) Make different lists with styles, musicians, instruments, etc.: things you know about popular urban music.
   b) Put numbers in your lists to classify your favourite styles, musicians and instruments.
   c) See the OLC to fill in the charts.
2. Ask me your questions.
   In pairs: make a list of questions (minimum 5, maximum 10) you would like to ask to learn about popular urban music in the unit.
   At the end of the unit we will check if you have learnt the answers to those questions.

FIND A CLASSMATE

1. After doing activity 1: Things I know and like about... Popular urban music, exchange your list with a classmate. Add some styles, musicians or instruments to the list.
2. Walk around and find a partner who has a similar order of preferences.

KEYWORDS

Make your own glossary throughout the unit. See the chart in the OLC and fill it in.

1 Popular Urban Music

1.1. Jazz: Free music

Jazz is the most important musical contribution to the history of music made by the United States.

This style was born at the beginning of the 20th century in New Orleans, in the heart of the community of African slaves brought centuries before. The slaves had their own ***work songs*** and also religious songs (***spirituals*** and ***gospel***) and the biggest contribution to the birth of jazz: the ***blues.*** The interaction of these manifestations and European music (dance orchestras, bands, etc.) created what we know today as jazz.

We can summarise the main characteristics of jazz in the following way:

- This style mainly uses ***improvisation.*** This is the instant, free creation of music.
- The structure of the compositions is usually around a main theme. We only hear this at the beginning and at the end. In the middle the musicians improvise, with some harmonies and in a certain number of bars.
- The rhythm is very important. The rhythms are very lively and there is usually a large variety of polyrhythms.
- 'Solos' are very important. These are passages where each musician does an improvisation, while the rest of the group performs in the background.

Jazz and other music extended rapidly through Europe thanks to the invention of the *gramophone* (Figure 8.1) and the *radio*.

These two inventions enormously helped music come to all audiences. They were also a revolution for the music industry and society in general. The creation of the record provided the possibility of listening to music at home and not only music performed live.

DID YOU KNOW?

The slaves tried to make their hard work in the cotton fields more tolerable with their **work songs** and **spirituals.**

Figure 8.1.
Inspired by the phonograph created by **Edison** in 1877, the *gramophone* was the first recorder/player in the history of the record. **Emile Berliner** invented it in 1888.

WORKSHEET

1. Answer the questions:
   a) Why were the gramophone and radio so important in the history of jazz and popular music?
   b) Who invented the gramophone?
   c) And the phonograph?
2. Download the activity 'Call Our Bluff'. Play with your classmates.

The most important musicians in the history of jazz include the singers **Louis Armstrong, Billie Holiday, Ella Fitzgerald** and the pianists **Thelonious Monk, Herbie Hancock, Chick Corea** and the Spanish **Tete Montolíu.** You will hear some of these musicians in the *Auditorium* section of this unit.

> **WORKSHEET**
>
> 3. Download and play the game 'A Word Beginning With...'.
>   a) ....style that contributed to the birth of jazz.
>   b) ...who is an important jazz musician.
>
>   Play this game with your partner and exchange the roles.

ACTIVITIES

1. **Now you can try your talent as a jazz musician by improvising with the recorder or glockenspiel over a blues piece.**

Blueseando

Here is a scale to help you. We use this scale a lot in this style. It has five notes and is called *pentatonic*:

Pentatonic scale

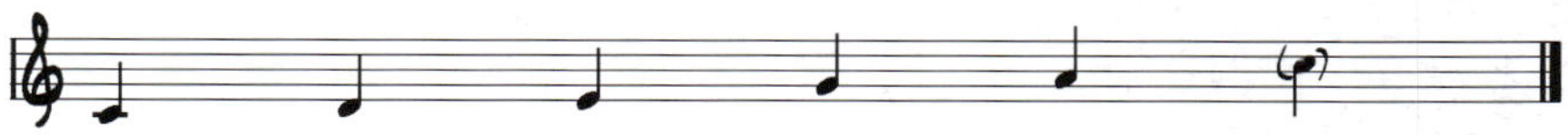

You can only use these five notes for your improvisation. First you will only use ♩ and later 𝅗𝅥; so you can make your improvisation as complex as you want.

You have two options to accompany your improvisation:

1. Class instruments, with your classmates accompanying you with the keyboard percussion instruments indicated in the score.
2. You can use the recorded backing track, with a blues piano accompaniment.

Figure 8.2.

B.B. King is one of the most famous blues guitarists and composers in history.

1.2. Rock And Roll: Power and Rhythm

Everything started with rock and roll (Figure 8.5). This style is one of the most important social and musical phenomena of the 20th century. It is the main vehicle of expression for many generations of youth.

Rock was born in the middle of the 20th century in the US. In its origins it directly built on blues and jazz.

But what is rock and roll? We can say it is strong, rhythmic music, made for dancing and free expression. This music must have a good singer, accompanied by the most authentic rock instrument: the *electric guitar* (Figure 8.3). It also has a *drum set* and a *bass guitar* (Figure 8.4).

The singer **Elvis Presley** (Figure 8.6) was the first musician dedicated to this style. With his popular hip movement and his energetic rock, he revolutionised the musical panorama of the fifties.

Figure 8.3.
Electric guitar: It played a fundamental role in the development of rock. **Leo Fender** designed the first electric guitar in the middle of the 20th century.

WORKSHEET

4. Download and complete the sentences.
5. Do fun OLC activities like Dancing, Singing Rock and Roll and Learning about Rock Instruments.

ACTIVITIES

2. Listen to a song by Elvis Presley, titled *Jailhouse Rock*. It is from the film of the same title, and Elvis also participated in it as the leading actor.

It is the story of a prisoner who learns to play the guitar in the prison. When he leaves, he becomes a rock star.

In the next decade, the sixties, rock and roll started progressively losing its function for dance, and the word rock on its own took form. **The Beatles** and **The Rolling Stones** were the main figures of rock. The Beatles included softer pop elements and The Rolling Stones made a more energetic rock style.

Figure 8.4.
Bass guitar: This instrument is similar to the electric guitar. The differences are that it has four strings that are thicker than the guitar's and a longer neck. This gives it a lower pitch.

Figure 8.5. A couple dancing rock and roll.

Figure 8.6. Elvis, the King of Rock and Roll.

The *hippie movement* began in the sixties. It rebelled against the established society and proposed ideals of peace and love for nature. Rock played a fundamental role in the extension of this movement, with artists like **Bob Dylan** (Figure 8.7), **Joan Baez, Jimi Hendrix, The Doors** and **The Who.**

WORKSHEET

6. Download and do the activity 'Match the Style and the Musician'.
7. Do the OLC 'Sing Along' activities and do some research about the hippie movement, Woodstock festival and share with your partner. See the links in the OLC.

Figure 8.7.
Bob Dylan is an American poet and musician. We consider him one of the most representative singer-songwriters of the 20th century.

The *Woodstock Festival* occurred in 1969 (Figure 8.8). We consider it the most emblematic concert of the decade. Almost all the great musicians of the time were there.

Figure 8.8.
The **Woodstock Festival** was also called the 'festival of flowers'.

ACTIVITIES

3. Listen to a part from the famous song *Knockin' on Heaven's Door*, by Bob Dylan. Many artists have made versions of it, including **Guns N' Roses** and **Eric Clapton.**

In the next decade, the seventies, the world of rock diversified enormously. Very different tendencies began: heavy metal was born, with bands like **AC/DC** and **Scorpions** (Figure 8.9). The precursor of this style was the British rock band **Led Zeppelin.**

Figure 8.9.
Heavy metal band Scorpions. Characteristics of heavy metal are the potent sound of distorted electric guitars, powerful drums and voices that sometimes scream. But we can also find quality ballads.

ACTIVITIES

4. Heavy metal bands are proud of composing the most beautiful ballads. Listen to one of the most famous ballads of the band Scorpions (Figure 8.9), ***Still Loving You.***

REMEMBER

Punk music is a type of rock with simple arrangements and a fast rhythm. It uses lyrics with political and social demands.

Punk was another important tendency of this period. Representative bands of this style are the **Sex Pistols** and **The Ramones.**

Symphonic rock bands also appeared during this period. This style uses elements of classical music, synthesisers, pianos, Hammond organs, etc. Representative bands of this variety of rock include **Emerson, Lake and Palmer, Pink Floyd, Genesis, Supertramp, Yes,** etc.

Another way of presenting music to the general public began in the eighties. This was the *music video,* a short musical film designed to promote songs and artists.

This technique gave musicians the possibility to show their work on television. Bands like **Dire Straits, U2, R.E.M., Guns N' Roses** and **Iron Maiden** triumphed during this decade.

In the nineties a new tendency emerged: *grunge*. This new style started in Seattle (USA) and was a mix of rock and punk, with a powerful sound and a rhythmic predominance of guitars. After the American band **Nirvana** made *Smells Like Teen Spirit,* grunge became one of the most relevant variations of rock of the entire decade. Other significant bands with this style were **Soundgarden** and **Pearl Jam.**

Now we have a significant element of rock called *alternative music* or *alternative rock*. We use this term to include bands that are not included in the more classical rock. They make their music for smaller audiences. But alternative music has elements of rock, pop, punk and grunge, without a sound that clearly differentiates it from traditional rock.

WORKSHEET

8. Think of a rock band or group on this page, but do not say the name. See the full explanation in the OLC.
9. Make a word search game about the subtypes of rock: punk, grunge, etc. Swap your work with another pair of classmates for them to solve.
10. Also make a matching activity to match a representative group with each substyle of rock.

1.3. Pop Music: Melody and Simplicity

Whereas rock has energetic power and rhythms, *pop music* has simple, catchy melodies that make us almost immediately start to sing.

One of its main characteristics is that it is made for large audiences. We use the same musical instruments, but the sound is much softer and less aggressive.

Pop music also emerged in the middle of the 20th century, directly from rock. They were both the first styles to benefit from the single.

Apart from **The Beatles** (Figure 8.10), there were other groups, like the Californian **The Beach Boys,** with their surfing philosophy and the beach as their symbol.

Figure 8.10.

The Beatles were a social and commercial revolution. They sold millions of copies, and even today their music is very present in our culture. There is even a videogame to give us the opportunity to experiment with their guitars, bass guitar, voices, etc.

Also coinciding with the hippie movement, in the sixties, was the American duo **Simon & Garfunkel.** They won three Grammy awards.

DID YOU KNOW?

The **single** was in its origin a vinyl disc with a short duration. It had one song on each side. Now in the world of radio, we use this term to designate a song which becomes a commercial success.

ACTIVITIES

5. **The appearance of The Beatles revolutionised the musical panorama of the sixties. They were at the top of the music charts and Beatlemania began. You can find many websites on the internet about this legendary band. Research a little more about them and try to discover:**
   - The names of the members and the part they had in the band.
   - The name of their first single.
   - The date the group disbanded.

   Listen to one of their songs, called *Can't Buy Me Love*.

WORKSHEET

11. Think of a pop band or group on this page, but do not say the name. See the full explanation in the OLC.
12. Make a word search game with your classmate and swap with another pair of classmates to guess the pop group.

WORKSHEET

13. Make a 'Who Am I?' activity about pop musicians or groups and ask your partner.

But the most important period of pop music was the eighties. During this time it became the most popular style, with musicians such as George Michael, Duran Duran, Spandau Ballet, New Kids on the Block and of course, **Michael Jackson** (Figure 8.11) and **Madonna.**

These musicians used the music video to launch their music hits, reaching record sales.

Today pop music is full of influences from very diverse music styles: electronic, Celtic, classical, Latin American, etc. It is difficult to identify this style with specific bands.

Figure 8.11.
***Thriller* by Michael Jackson:** This video clip established a new way of doing music videos. You can see part of this video on the internet.

1.4. Pop and Rock in Spain

At the end of the Franco's dictatorship, Spanish pop and rock were born as a way of expressing the transition toward democracy.

The *movida madrileña* emerged during these years. This cultural movement started in the capital of Spain and manifested itself in music, painting, photography, literature and cinema.

This *movida* rapidly extended to other parts of the country, causing the rise of Spanish pop and rock.

This movement included artists such as the film maker **Pedro Almodóvar, Alaska** (Figure 8.12), **Gabinete Caligari, Radio Futura, Mecano, La Unión, Nacha Pop, Los Secretos** and **Loquillo.**

Figure 8.12.
Alaska, Spanish pop icon.

ACTIVITIES

6. The song you will listen to became a Spanish pop icon. It is from the band **Burning** and it is called *¿Qué hace una chica como tú en un sitio como este?*

2 Auditorium: Jazz

A. The Facts

Jazz emerged in the black population of New Orleans. It was a combination of musical elements present there: the ***African-American tradition,*** *spirituals* and ***music of the white population,*** with its military bands and dance orchestras of European origin. One of the characteristics of jazz is ***improvisation.*** This is the creation of music at the moment we play it.

Between 1870 and 1930 the very first foundations of jazz as we know it today were established. ***Ragtime*** was a piano style that combines dance music with the *banjo* technique. ***Blues*** was the expression of the slaves' pain and suffering and the foundation for the first jazz ever. ***Dixieland*** style was the early imitation that the white musicians did of New Orleans jazz. *Chicago* was the style of one of the most charismatic jazz musicians of all times, **Louis Armstrong** (Figure 8.13).

After 1930, other styles appeared. ***Swing*** was the style which commercialised jazz. The groups grew to become *big bands,* and were like a big show. Swing dominated dance music and the cinema. ***Bebop*** was experimental jazz which broke with the previous danceable style. ***Cool jazz*** was the reaction to the intellectual style of bebop. ***Free jazz*** was close to contemporary music and far from traditional jazz elements. Finally, there was ***fusion,*** a mix of jazz with other styles, like rock or flamenco.

Figure 8.13.
Louis Armstrong, jazz composer and trumpet player.

WORKSHEET

14. Miles Davis and John Coltrane.
    a) Who do you like most? Why?
    b) What instruments did they play?
    c) Where did they live?

B. The music 7

Next we will go through the sounds that made jazz a vibrant, constantly evolving music.

- **Scott Joplin,** famous for his ragtime. Listen to a part of *The Entertainer.* It appeared in the film *The Sting.*
- **Louis Armstrong,** trumpet player and singer. His recordings set the foundations for later jazz. Listen to his version of *Mack the Knife.*
- **Glenn Miller,** from the world of swing and big bands. *In the Mood* has some of the most famous orchestral *riffs* (musical phrases that are repeated) of jazz music.
- **Charlie Parker:** Listen to an excerpt from *Ornithology.*
- **Miles Davis** (Figure 8.14). He participated in bebop, cool, vanguard and even in fusion with rock and flamenco. Listen to *Rocker,* from the album *Birth of the Cool.*
- We consider **Chick Corea** one of the greatest jazz pianists since 1960. He fused jazz with other styles and felt a predilection for Spanish music. Listen to *Night Streets,* from the album *My Spanish Heart.*

Figure 8.14.
Miles Davis, trumpet player and one of the most influential figures in the history of jazz.

3 A Lot of Rhythm

WORKSHEET

15. See the glossary: useful expressions in regard to rhythm.

In this lesson we will study the *quaver triplet:*

The triplet is an 'irregular group'. It substitutes two equal figures for three of the same type. It divides the crotchet into three quavers, instead of two.

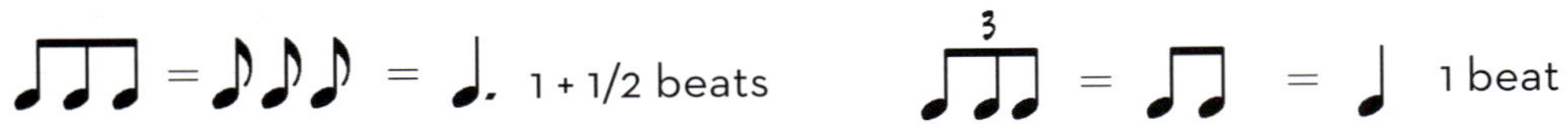

Exercise 1

Repeating exercise: listen to each rhythm in one bar and then repeat it.

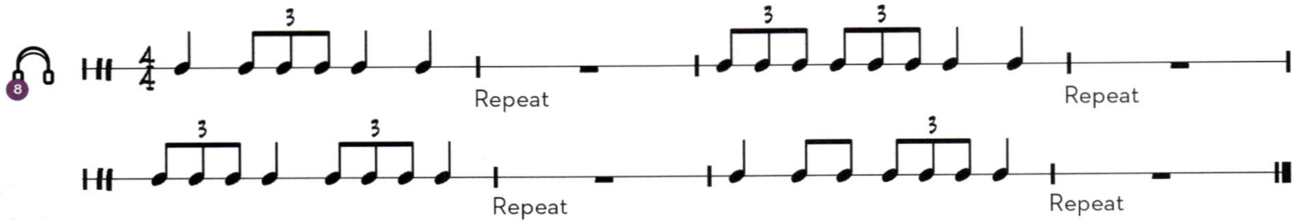

Exercise 2

Exercise 3

Do the following exercise with body percussion:

Exercise 4

Practise the following drum pattern:

4 In Tune

A. Reading Music

We add the E note on the fourth space of the stave to those you already worked on.

B. Repertoire

We will sing a song by the band Mecano. You listened to it in Unit 4 of your book, in two versions. It is the song *Hijo de la luna*. Sing it over the accompaniment and be careful to stay in tune and project your voice we l.

WORKSHEET

16. See the glossary: useful expressions in regard to tuning your voice.

Tonto el que no entienda.
Cuenta una leyenda
que una hembra gitana
conjuró a la luna
hasta el amanecer.
Llorando pedía
al llegar el día
desposar un calé.
Tendrás a tu hombre,
piel morena,
desde el cielo
habló la luna llena.
Pero a cambio quiero
el hijo primero
que le engendres a él.
Que quien su hijo inmola
para no estar sola
poco le iba a querer.

CHORUS

Luna quieres ser madre
y no encuentras querer
que te haga mujer.
Dime, luna de plata,
qué pretendes hacer
con un niño de piel.
A-ha-ha-ha, a-ha-ha-ha,
hijo de la luna.

De padre canela
nació un niño
blanco como el lomo
de un armiño,
con los ojos grises
en vez de aceituna
niño albino de luna.
«¡Maldita su estampa!
este hijo es de un payo
y yo no me lo callo.»

CHORUS

Gitano al creerse deshonrado,
se fue a su mujer,
cuchillo en mano.
«¿De quién es el hijo?
Me has engañao' fijo.»
y de muerte la hirió.
Luego se hizo al monte
con el niño en brazos
y allí le abandonó.

CHORUS

Y las noches
que haya luna llena
será porque el niño
esté de buenas.
Y si el niño llora
menguará la luna
para hacerle una cuna.
Y si el niño llora
menguará la luna
para hacerle una cuna.

Figure 8.15.
Mecano, an icon of eighties pop music.

5 Move Your Fingers

WORKSHEET

17. See the glossary: useful expressions in regard to playing the recorder.

In this unit we will add three new elements: the *mordent*, the *trill* and the *F sharp* note.

The **mordent** (~) is a rapid single alternation of the upper note. To play it on the recorder, we will lift our finger rapidly and immediately place it over the original note.

To play the **trill** (tr~~) we will rapidly alternate the original note with the upper one. The resulting effect is similar the sound of a bird.

In the unit resources we will hear the following backgrounds:

- *Accompaniment for exercises 1 and 2:* We can hear the following traditional instruments of Japan and China: *koto, taiko drums* and *shakuhachi* (Figure 8.16).
- *Accompaniment for exercises 3 and 4:* You will hear the *pan flute* (Figure 8.17) in this recording.

Exercise 1

Exercise 2

Exercise 3

Exercise 4

Figure 8.16.
Shakuhachi: Japanese vertical flute made from bamboo.

Figure 8.17.
Pan flute: Made from several cane tubes; each one is for a different note.

6 Concert

The piece you will play now is dedicated to one of the greatest jazz musicians of all times, **Duke Ellington.** Pianist, composer and orchestra conductor, Edward Kennedy Ellington was born in Washington, D.C. on 29 April 1899.

He started to study piano at 7 years old. He formed an orchestra and its members accompanied him for many years. They played in the *Cotton Club* from 1927 to 1932. They were so successful that when they went on their first European tour in 1933, it was the most famous orchestra in the world. Ellington went on tours until his death in 1974. He received numerous honours and distinctions.

Big 'Duke' Band

15 16

Music: José Palazón

Figure 8.18.

Duke Ellington at the piano in an improvisation session.

Download and print the worksheet you will find in the OLC to complete the concept map of the unit.

- **Popular urban music**
  - **Jazz**
    - B … — A … slaves in the U … sang w … songs.
    - J … — This style comes from the b …. Its main characteristic is i ….
  - **R …**
    - Rock and roll — R …, powerful music for d ….
    - Sixties — Influence from the h … movement in music.
    - Seventies and eighties — New tendencies in rock: …, h … metal, s … rock, etc.
    - Nineties — G …. A … rock.
  - **P …**
    - Characteristics — Simple, c … melodies. We use the same i … as in rock, but in a s … way.
  - **Pop and rock in Spain**
    - *M … madrileña* — This favoured the r … of rock and pop in Spain.

FINAL ACTIVITIES

1. In your Workbook, write the main characteristics of jazz that you have studied in the unit.
2. List the musical instruments that are mostly used in jazz music.
3. Name four famous jazz musicians.
4. Who designed the first electric guitar?
5. Define heavy metal and punk in your Workbook.
6. Below are the names of various music artists and bands. In your Workbook, match each one of them with their corresponding style.

MUSICIANS	STYLES
Scorpions •	• Symphonic rock
Louis Armstrong •	• Spanish pop
Nirvana •	• Grunge
Rolling Stones •	• Rock
Nacha Pop •	• Jazz
Genesis •	• Heavy metal

7. Complete the following sentences with information from this unit:
   - Work songs were songs that ... .
   - Jazz musicians improvise, especially in the ... part of the ... piece.
   - The first device that could record and play music was called ... .
   - The main rock instruments are the electric guitar, ... and ... .
   - The band **Pearl Jam** is a ... group.
   - One of the most famous music videos in the history of pop was ... by ... .

8. In your Workbook, write the names of your favourite rock, pop, hip hop, etc., bands. Choose the one you like the most and write a brief paragraph about it.
9. Name other styles of popular urban music that were described in other units of the book and not in this one.
10. Do you like the idea of creating a music band with your friends? Do you know what to do for this? Write the steps to follow in your workbook.

11. **Read the article on music piracy below. Debate this topic in class in an organised way. You can use the following questions as a guide.**

- How do you think music piracy affects musicians and the music industry?
- Where do you think the problem comes from? Do you think CDs are too expensive?
- Do you think music piracy is a problem for music in general? Or do you think musicians will continue creating music?
- Can you think of a solution?

Music piracy: a mortal virus?

Today the music industry faces its worst enemy in all of history: music piracy. This phenomenon occurs through internet file sharing programmes and street selling of pirated CDs.

The price difference in comparison with the original CD and especially the easiness of receiving free music at home has caused computer P2P programmes to be installed in most homes with internet access. Profits have decreased for large record companies. Consequently, musicians have earned less money. Small record companies cannot continue their business.

The situation has reached a point where some of the large record companies study the economic viability of giving their music through free downloads on their own websites and obtaining profits only through advertisements inserted on these websites.

FINAL PROJECT

1. Choose a famous rock, pop or jazz song you like on YouTube. Search for other performers playing the same song and explain the differences between the different covers.
2. You can use criteria to compare them like: tempo, duration, instruments, variation in melody, number of solos, musical style, form or structure, texture, (all the elements of music you have studied throughout this book) and other subjective characteristics like: originality, creativity, etc.
3. Fill in the chart in the OLC.
4. You should choose a very well-known song so that it has a large variety of covers.
5. You can use a similar chart in the OLC.

   You can also add some extra information about the different performers of the same song, or interesting information about the composition of this song, the lyrics, etc.
6. Present the covers to your classmates and teacher through a PowerPoint presentation.

   Of course, we will listen to the different covers while you explain your comparison.
7. Assess your other classmates' projects.

9 MUSICAL FOLKLORE

Throughout history, music has always been part of our lives, accompanying us in our daily routines, in our festivities, celebrations and all types of social and religious events.

This music emerges from the people, from our tradition, connected to our preferences and customs. Every culture, nation or region, from any place in the world, has a music that identifies it. This music expresses its peculiarities and characteristics. This is the musical folklore.

In this unit we will study the rich and varied Spanish musical folklore. We will learn about it and respect it as part of our cultural heritage.

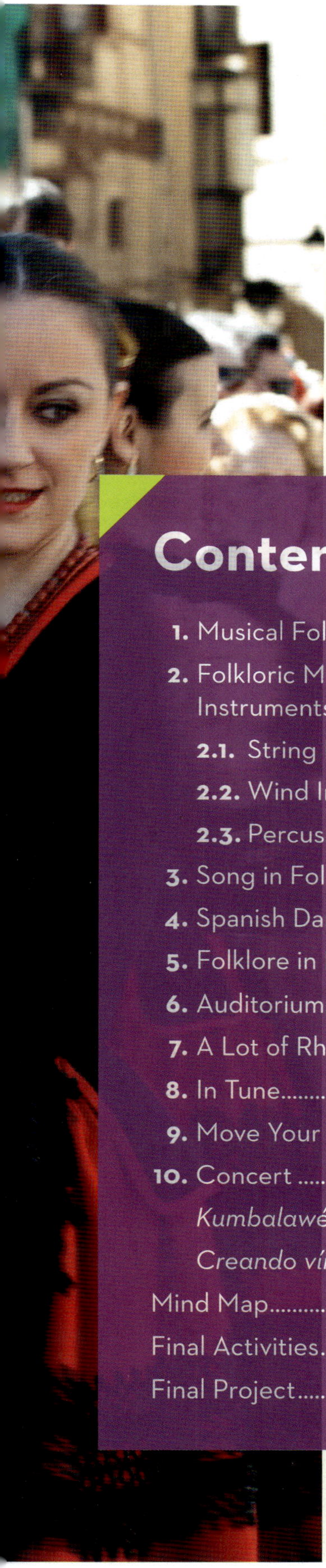

Contents

WORK ON THE TEXT

Download the worksheet and fill in the gaps.

1. Why has music been a part of our lives?
2. What is musical folklore?
3. What are we going to learn in this unit?

WARM UP

Things I know about... folk music.

1. Make different lists with musicians, instruments, etc...: things you know about folk music from your region, other regions of Spain or from other countries. See the diagram in the OLC to fill in.
2. Learn something else.

   Now try to show your knowledge about Spanish musical folklore in the online activity.

   Did you get the right answer?

FIND A CLASSMATE

Discussion.

1. Have you ever seen a folkloric dance, music performance, etc.? When and where?
2. Do you think that it is important to know and preserve folklore?
3. Discuss in pairs and write 2 reasons for this.
4. Do you know somebody who takes part in a folk group dancing, playing or singing?

KEYWORDS

Make your own glossary for the unit. See the chart in the OLC to fill in.

1 Musical Folklore

DID YOU KNOW?

The origins of the term *folklore* go back to the middle of the 19th century. It comes from **folk** (people) and **lore** (science) and refers to the set of manifestations of the traditional culture of a people.

RESOURCES WEB

You can find more information about **Manuel de Falla** on the resources website.

We use the term **folklore** for the traditions, customs and popular beliefs of a certain geographical area (town, country, region, etc.). So we can say folklore is Argentinean, Hungarian, Valencian, etc.

In this unit we will learn more about our musical *folklore: the traditional songs, dances and instruments* that are characteristic of our country. Throughout the centuries, Spain was inhabited by different people and cultures. These gave us most of our musical tradition, making Spanish musical folklore one of the most diverse and rich in the world.

There are a series of common characteristics in all the manifestations of *traditional music*, independently of where they are from:

- **Function:** It accompanies all types of activities (agricultural work, housework, games, festivities, etc.).
- **Anonymity:** The authors' names are not known and we consider them the product of the entire group.
- **Oral transmission:** from generation to generation. This makes them adapt and transform throughout history. But this is also a problem because we lose many of them over time. Folklore experts recover and compile a lot of material. This allows us to learn about the music that accompanied our ancestors and still survives today.

Figure 9.1.
We can find very diverse folklore manifestations in the world.

Musical folklore was also a source of inspiration for *art music*. Traditional music inspired many composers when composing some of their pieces, as with the Spaniard **Manuel de Falla.** The popular melodies and rhythms of traditional music were the basis for many pieces of music. This had its maximum expression in *musical nationalism* of the 19th and 20th centuries, where music was a medium for increasing patriotism.

WORKSHEET

1. Download and write the correct text question.
2. True or false activity. See the OLC for the whole explanation.

ACTIVITIES

1. What do you know about the folklore of where you live? Research and write a little summary about the customs and traditions of your area. You can write about local festivities or typical foods, explain characteristic expressions or phrases, etc.

2 Folkloric Musical Instruments

There is a large variety of traditional instruments in the Spanish territory. These are the instruments we use in folkloric music.

Some of them are present all around the Iberian Peninsula, and some are more characteristic of certain areas. We grouped them by families to make them easier to study.

2.1. String Instruments

The most popular instrument is the *guitar*. We usually associate it with Andalusian folklore, but it is present in all Spanish traditional music. The *guitar*, the *lute* and the *bandurria* are usually present in *rondallas*. These are musical ensembles that are very characteristic of Spanish folkloric music. The instruments of these ensembles are mainly string instruments.

Other traditional instruments include the *chicotén* (Figure 9.2); the *hurdy-gurdy* (Figure 9.3, *viola de roda*), characteristic of Galicia; the *Canarian timple* (Figure 9.4), similar to the guitar, but smaller and with fewer strings; and the *rabel* (Figure 9.5), a type of violin of Arabian heritage.

WORKSHEET

3. Guess My Word: download and write the activity.

   Think of a folk string instrument, don't say it and stand up.

   See the OLC for the whole explanation.

4. A Word Beginning With: prepare your list of string instruments from every Spanish region.

   Download the whole explanation.

Figure 9.2.
We play the ***chicotén*** by striking its strings with a drumstick. They call it *salterio* (psaltery) in Castile-La Mancha and *tun-tun* in the Basque Country.

Figure 9.3.
The **hurdy-gurdy** *(viola de roda)* is a medieval instrument played by two people. They held it on their legs. One turned the wheel and the other operated the keys.

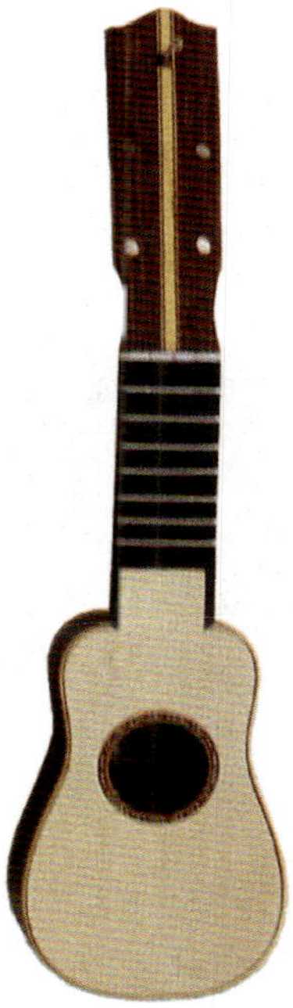

Figure 9.4.
The **Canarian timple** is a musical instrument from the Canary Islands. It is small and can have four or five strings.

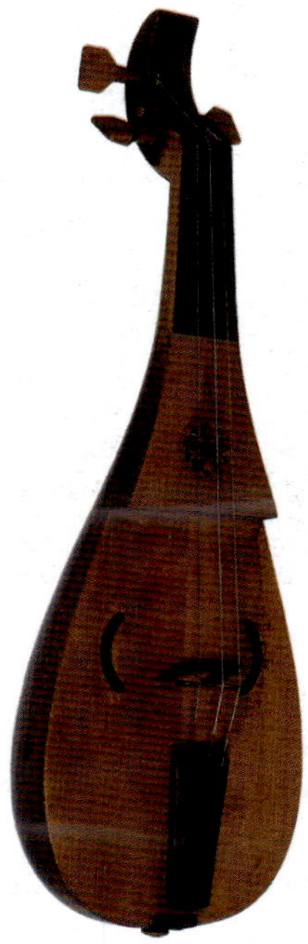

Figure 9.5.
The ***rabel*** is a bowed string instrument. The Arabs probably brought it to the peninsula.

Figure 9.6. The ***txistu.***

Figure 9.7. The ***flabiol.***

Figure 9.8. The ***alboka.***

2.2. Wind Instruments

We obtain sound in a similar way to the woodwind instruments we studied in Unit 5. These include:

- ***Flutes*** (like the recorder): the *Basque txistu* (Figure 9.6) and the Catalan *flabiol* (Figure 9.7). The *flabiol* is part of the *coblas* (traditional musical ensembles of Catalonia). They also use it in the Balearic Islands.
- ***Single-reed instruments*** (like the clarinet): the *alboka* (Figure 9.8) is typical of the Basque Country.
- ***Double-reed instruments*** (like the oboe): the *dulzaina* (Figure 9.9), very common in the peninsula (Castile and León, Castile-La Mancha, Valencia and Aragon), and the *chirimía.*

An instrument used a lot in brass bands and carnivals is the *mirliton* or *kazoo.* It has a hollow reed that is perforated in the centre and covered with rolling paper tied with a string. When we hum into it, the paper vibrates and modifies the sound.

We cannot finish this section without mentioning the bagpipes *(gaitas).* We normally associate them with Celtic music, but their origin is not clear. Their use is very extended, not only in the Spanish territory, but in many other parts of the world. In Spain these include the Galician and Asturian bagpipes.

The bagpipes (Figure 9.10) have a goatskin bag that stores air. We blow air through a small tube or mouthpiece. This has an internal valve to prevent air from going out. When we press the goatskin bag, the air goes out through two pipes. One is a conical tube with holes. In the upper part of this tube there is a double-reed pipe that vibrates. The other one is a long, cylindrical tube with a single reed. This produces a sustained note which harmonises with the melody played on the conical tube.

WORKSHEET

5. Guess My Word: download and write the activity.

   Think of a folk wind instrument, don't say it and stand up.

   See the OLC for the whole explanation.
6. A Word Beginning With: prepare your list of wind instruments from every Spanish region. Download the whole explanation.

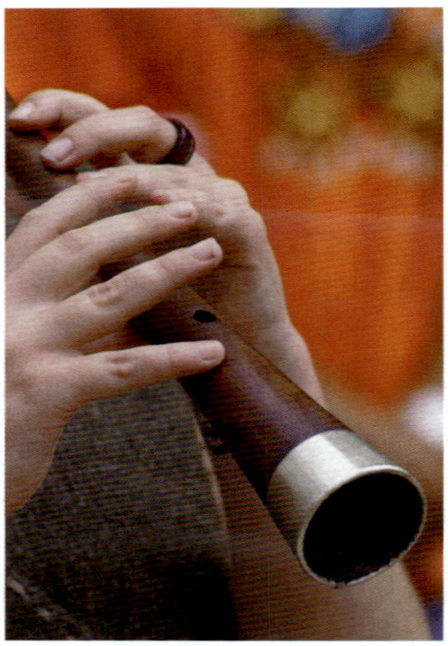

Figure 9.9. The ***dulzaina.***

Figure 9.10. The **bagpipes *(gaitas).***

2.3. Percussion Instruments

Percussion instruments are the most abundant and diverse traditional instruments in our folklore. You know some of them already, like the *castanets* (with different variations like the Murcian *postizas* and the Canarian *chácaras*) the cowbell *(cencerro)* and the *tambourine* (*pandero*, which can be round or square).

Another instrument that is very common all around the peninsula is the *tamboril* or small snare drum (Figure 9.12). There are different varieties of sizes. Originally they accompanied it with a three-holed flute.

Other instruments include the *carraca* or ratchet (Figure 9.13) and the *matraca*, used a lot during Holy Week; the *arrabel* or *huesera*, made up of a set of reeds, sticks or bones tied together which sound when rubbed by a castanet; the *zambomba* or friction drum (Figure 9.14), used a lot during Christmas or Carnival; and the *txalaparta* (Figure 9.15), a very typical instrument of Navarre and the Basque Country.

Finally, the use of certain everyday objects or utensils as percussion instruments is also very frequent in traditional music. Examples are the *mortar* and the *anisette bottle*.

Figure 9.11.

Drum festivals: Thousands of people come together to play drums simultaneously during Holy Week in some places of Albacete and Murcia (Hellín, Mula, etc.).

Figure 9.12. The ***tamboril.***

Figure 9.13. The ***carraca.***

Figure 9.14. The ***zambomba.***

Figure 9.15. The ***txalaparta.***

WORKSHEET

7. Guess My Word: download and write the activity.

   Think of a percussion instrument, don't say it and stand up. See the OLC for the whole explanation.

8. A Word Beginning With: prepare your list of percussion instruments from every Spanish region. Download the whole explanation.

3 Song in Folklore

The songs of Spanish musical folklore have a lot of rhythm and rich melodies. The themes are very diverse. Here are some of the most representative types:

- **Christmas carols:** Like *villancicos* and *aguinaldos*.
- **Carnival songs:** The lyrics criticise and ridicule certain aspects of the current social reality with humour and irony. For example, there are *chirigotas* (Figure 9.17) from Cádiz and *murgas* from the Canary Islands.
- **Work songs:** Used especially for agricultural work (harvesting).
- **Lullabies:** Melodies to make small children sleep. There are different names in the different regions: *arroró, nana, añada, lo-kantak* (the Basque Country) and de *bresol* (Majorca).
- **Children's songs:** To accompany games (in a ring, jumping rope, etc.).
- **Serenades:** Young people express their love with these songs. They accompany their singing with a *rondalla* (*bandurrias*, guitars, lutes, etc.).
- **Wedding songs** or *alboradas:* They sing these during the early morning of the wedding to the bride, groom and wedding attendants.
- **Religious songs:** Like *ramos, romerías, salves* and prayer songs (to ask the Virgin Mary and the saints for rain or a good harvest).
- ***Quintos* songs:** *Quintos* were young men of the same age who had to do military service. Before leaving, they came together to serenade the young women of the town. They composed and sang songs especially for the occasion.

CURIOUS FACTS

In Andalusia and Extremadura there are groups of ***campanilleros,*** who sing religious songs with guitars, bells and other instruments.

In the region of Murcia there are brotherhoods of ***Auroros.*** They go out to sing on early Sunday mornings *(despiertas)* or singing nights. They sing songs to venerate the Virgin Mary, Christ and the saints, and accompany them with bells.

DID YOU KNOW?

We compile popular songs in books called **song books.**

WORKSHEET

9. In groups make a mind map with all the different types of songs and their subtypes by regions.

   See the OLC for the whole explanation.

10. Define the different song genres to your classmate.

Figure 9.16. *Chirigota* from Cádiz.

4 Spanish Dance

Since early times, dance has always been present in the life of humans. It is connected to our customs, celebrations and traditions. Spain has a lot of folkloric dances. Some are common among different geographical areas, with their own exclusive singularities from each region. Here are some of them:

> **WORKSHEET**
>
> 11. Match the dance with the region in the OLC map.
> 12. Go to the website. Learn, write and compare in the OLC chart.

Figure 9.17. Typical folkloric dances from the different Spanish regions.

ACTIVITIES

2. **As you see, we have a large variety of dances, and these are only the most representative. Now research one of the dances above or a different one from your autonomous community.**

   Discover its origin, musical characteristics, the musical instruments that accompany it, what the dance is like (number of dancers, steps, etc.), typical clothes, etc.

> **DID YOU KNOW?**
>
> In Spain there are a lot of **choirs and dance groups** and national and international folklore festivals. These contribute to extending the diverse and rich folklore of the towns of Spain and other countries.

5 Folklore in Modern Music

Figure 9.18.
We consider **Carlos Núñez** one of the best bagpipe players in the world.

Today many elements of traditional music are present in rock and pop. New musical tendencies emerged with the popular melodies and rhythms of folk music and its instruments. These are now very important.

In general we refer to this type of music as *folk music,* world music or ethnic music, but the terminology and classifications used are a little confusing.

There are a large number of folk groups in Spain. The following are some examples:

- **Milladoiro**

  This is one of the most emblematic Galician musical ensembles. It began at the end of the seventies. Now it has seven members.

- **Carlos Núñez** (Figure 9.18)

  We consider him one of the most expert *bagpipe players* in the world. He started to play the bagpipes when he was eight years old. He collaborates with several musicians and artists, like the Chieftains, and fuses Celtic music with very different styles like flamenco, pop, Arab and Jewish music.

- **Kepa Junkera**

  He is a Basque musician and virtuoso on the *trikitixa* (diatonic accordion). He mixes the musical tradition of the Basque Country with other music, like jazz, classical music and folk music from other parts of the world.

- **Luar na Lubre** (Figure 9.20)

  This group started out strong on the folk and traditional Galician music scene in 1986. It became famous in 1992 when the famous British musician of Irish descent, Mike Oldfield, became interested in their music.

WORKSHEET

13. Make a 'Who Am I?' question about folk musicians or groups and ask your partner. Swap.
14. 'Student Generated Word Puzzle' with famous folk musicians and groups.

    Download and see the full explanation.

DID YOU KNOW?

When talking about folklore in today's music, we must also mention Radio Tarifa in Andalusia, the Asturian Llan de Cubel, Música Nostra in the Balearic Islands, the Canarian Mestisay, Gaiteros del Faro in Cantabria, La Musgaña or Nuevo Mester de Juglaría in Castile and León, Manantial Folk in Extremadura and the Murcian Azarbe.

Figure 9.19.
The Irish band the **Chieftains.**
A large part of the folk music made in Spain, mainly in the north of the peninsula, comes from Celtic music. This type of music has its foundation in the folk music of regions of Irish descent (like Ireland, Scotland, Wales, Britain, Galicia, Asturias, etc.).

ACTIVITIES

3. Listen to a part from the traditional Basque song *Maitia nun zira*. **Kepa Junkera** and the singer **Dulce Pontes** performed this version. You can find the lyrics and their translation on the website.

4. Play the following compositions on the recorder. The first is the traditional Basque song you heard in a version by **Kepa Junkera** and the second is the famous song O son do ar by the Galician folk group **Luar na Lubre.**

Figure 9.20.
Luar na Lubre is one of the most important folk ensembles in Galicia.

Figure 9.21.
Kepa Junkera, composer, producer and musician born in Bilbao.

Maitia nun zira

Traditional Basque song

O son do ar

Luar na Lubre

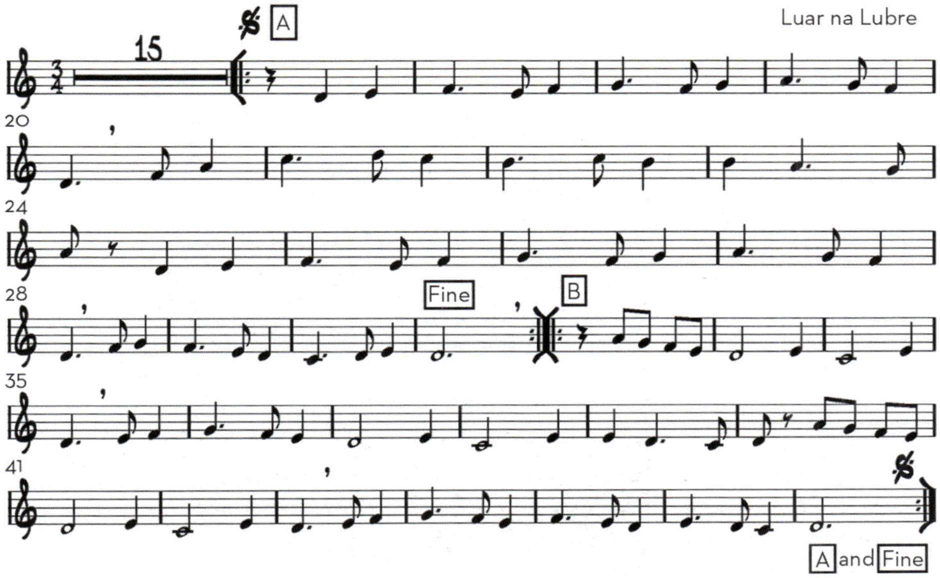

6 Auditorium: Flamenco

A. The Facts

Figure 9.22.
The three main elements of flamenco: dancing, singing and playing (Spanish guitar).

We will finish the *Auditorium* section with one of the most internationally relevant Spanish musical contributions: *flamenco*.

But **what** exactly **is** flamenco? How did it emerge and how did it develop? When we refer to flamenco, we mean that it is a type of popular music and dance practised in Andalusia. It is present in three basic forms: ***dancing, singing* and *guitar playing*** (Figure 9.22).

Its art comes from numerous **influences** that diverse cultures left when they lived in the south of the peninsula. These are the Christian, Arab, Jewish and Gypsy cultures.

Figure 9.23.
Paco de Lucía, one of the greatest references in flamenco guitar.

During the middle of the 19th century an art form called *flamenco* emerged from this cultural mix. Gradually it moved from its performance in gypsy families to the ***tablaos.*** Currently, flamenco is highly-valued and performed in the most important auditoriums of the world.

Flamenco is **classified** in *palos*, differing by the sad or happy character and in their rhythmic composition. The most primitive ***palos*** are the *seguidillas, soleares, bulerías, saetas, rumbas, fandangos* and *tangos*.

B. The Music

Now we will listen to musical excerpts from three important musicians of this music trend:

- **Camarón de la Isla** was one of the main *cantaores* (flamenco singers) in the history of flamenco. You will hear a part of his song *Soy gitano* from the album with the same name.
- **Paco de Lucía** (Figure 9.23) was the most internationally famous flamenco guitarist. One of his greatest contributions was to enrich flamenco with influences from jazz, blues and popular music. Listen to his guitar in the next fragment. You can also hear the typical flamenco clapping.
- The pianist and composer **Chano Domínguez** fuses flamenco with jazz. He obtains a characteristic language from the mix of different flamenco *palos* as a complement to his rich jazz improvisations. Listen to the following excerpt from the song *Retahíla*, from the album *Hecho a mano*.

WORKSHEET

15. Activity 'Write the Correct Question'. See the full explanation in the OLC.

RESOURCES WEB

You can find more information about flamenco on the website.

7 A Lot of Rhythm

In this lesson we will study the rhythmic formula: 

This formula substitutes the second *quaver* for two *semiquavers*. When we studied quavers, we used the syllables *ti-ti* and for semiquavers *ti-ri-ti-ri*. We will combine these in the following way:

Figure 9.24.
The *cajón* is a symbol of rhythmic accompaniment to the flamenco style.

Do the following rhythm exercises by clapping or tapping your knees, alternating hands. You can also use rhythm syllables. Then do them with the recording.

Exercise 1

Exercise 2

WORKSHEET

16. See the glossary: useful expressions in regard to rhythm.

Practise this polyrhythm by tapping both hands on your knees. You can also do it with bongos.

Exercise 3

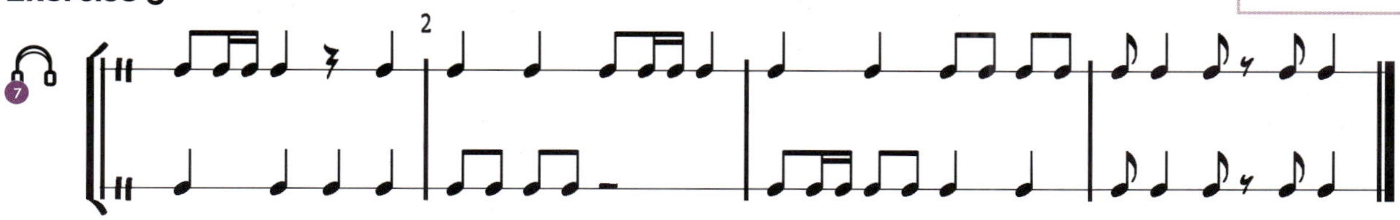

Exercise 4

Practise the following drum pattern.

WORKSHEET

17. See the glossary: useful expressions in regard to singing.

8 In Tune

A. Reading Music

We will add the F note on the 5th line of the stave to those you already worked on.

B. Repertoire

In this unit we will sing a nice song called *Sing*, with music from Gary Barlow and Andrew Lloyd Webber. You can work on the pronunciation and translation of the lyrics before singing it.

Figure 9.25.
Scene from the musical *Cats*, by the composer **Andrew Lloyd Webber,** famous for composing the music for legendary musicals, like *Jesus Christ Superstar* and *The Phantom of the Opera*.

Solo: Some words they can't be spoken only sung,
So hear a thousand voices shouting love.

Backing vocals: There's a place, there's a time
In this life when you sing what you are feeling,
Find your feet, stand your ground,
Don't you see
Right now the world is listening to what we say?

CHORUS
Sing it louder, sing it clearer,
Knowing everyone will hear you,
Make some noise, find your voice tonight.
Sing it stronger, sing together,
Make this moment last forever,
Old and young
Shouting love tonight.

To sing we've had a lifetime to wait
And see a thousand faces celebrate
You brought hope, you brought light,
Conquered fear, it wasn't always easy,
Stood your ground, kept your faith,
Don't you see
Right now the world is listening to what we say?

Sing it louder, sing it clearer,
Knowing everyone will hear you,
Make some noise, find your voice tonight.
Sing it stronger, sing together,
Make this moment last forever,
Old and young
Shouting love tonight.

Some words they can't be spoken only sung,
To hear a thousand voices shouting love
And light and hope

Just sing (x 4)
Come all and sing

Sing it louder, sing it clearer,
Knowing everyone will hear you,
Make some noise, find your voice tonight.
Sing it stronger, sing together,
Make this moment last forever,
Old and young
Shouting love tonight.

Solo: Hear a thousand voices shouting love.

Listen to a version of this song sung by a secondary school choir.

9 Move Your Fingers

This last section of *Move Your Fingers* is dedicated to melodic pop music with a symphonic orchestra *(Exercises 1 and 2)* and one of the most representative manifestations of Brazilian music: the *samba (Exercises 3 and 4)*.

Exercise 1

Exercise 2

Exercise 3

Exercise 4

WORKSHEET

18. See the glossary: useful expressions in regard to playing the recorder.

The **samba** is a type of Brazilian music originally from Africa. It is famous around the world because of the carnival in Río de Janeiro (Figure 9.26).

A very special ensemble for playing this music is the *batucada*. This is an orchestra composed exclusively of percussion instruments. It accompanies the Brazilian carnival parades. Some common instruments in the *batucada* are the *surdo*, the *caixa de guerra*, the *agogo* and the *tamborim*.

Figure 9.26.
We consider the **Río de Janeiro carnival** the mecca of the samba.

WORKSHEET

19. Download, answer and discuss.
    a) What is the samba?
    b) What is a batucada?
    c) What are the main instruments in a batucada?
    d) Have you ever seen a batucada in your city?
    e) Do you like instruments and rhythms in the batucada?

Share your opinions and experiences with your partner.

10 Concert

Figure 9.27.
Member of the **Cirque du Soleil** during a performance.

The **Cirque du Soleil** (Figures 9.27 - 9.29) is a company founded in Canada in 1984. Since its origin, this group has tried to reinvent the circus. It creates its own style where spectacular acrobatics, evocative scenography and original music create a beautiful show. Its basic premise is innovation, creativity, delicacy and not using wild animals in their shows.

Different productions travel around Europe, Japan and South America. They have won over a hundred awards.

The song you will hear for this last Concert section is from the *Saltimbanco* show of the Cirque du Soleil. It is called *Kumbalawé*. You will alternate between **singing** and **playing the recorder** as you prepare and later perform this piece.

RESOURCES WEB

You will find the complete original song on the resources website.

Steps for preparing *Kumbalawé*

1. **Listen** carefully to an excerpt of the original song several times.
2. Practise **singing the lyrics** you find on the website with the original song. You can divide the class into two groups, soloists and backing vocals, to interpret the piece like the original song.
3. Practise the **recorder part separately.**
4. After practising several times, you can now **perform the piece with the recorded accompaniment.** Be careful with the parts you sing and play with the recorder. You will find the indications in the *music diagram* on the next page.

Figure 9.28.
Several members of the show *Saltimbanco*.

Figure 9.29.
The costumes are some of the most significant elements of this show. They combine with innovative scenography.

Kumbalawé

Music: René Duperé

Figure 9.30.
Many of the members of the Cirque du Soleil are former elite athletes. There are artists from over forty countries.

MUSIC DIAGRAM

Recorder	Lyrics	Recorder	Lyrics	Lyrics	Coda
Section **A**	**Soloist-backing vocals**	Sections **A** and **B**	**Backing vocals**	**Soloist-backing vocals**	Phrase 1 × 2 times Phrase 2 × 4 times and end

Now you will use class instruments. *Creando vínculos* is a composition with a minimalist and melodic style. The entire group working together will give a very satisfactory musical performance.

Creando vínculos

Music: José Luis Salas

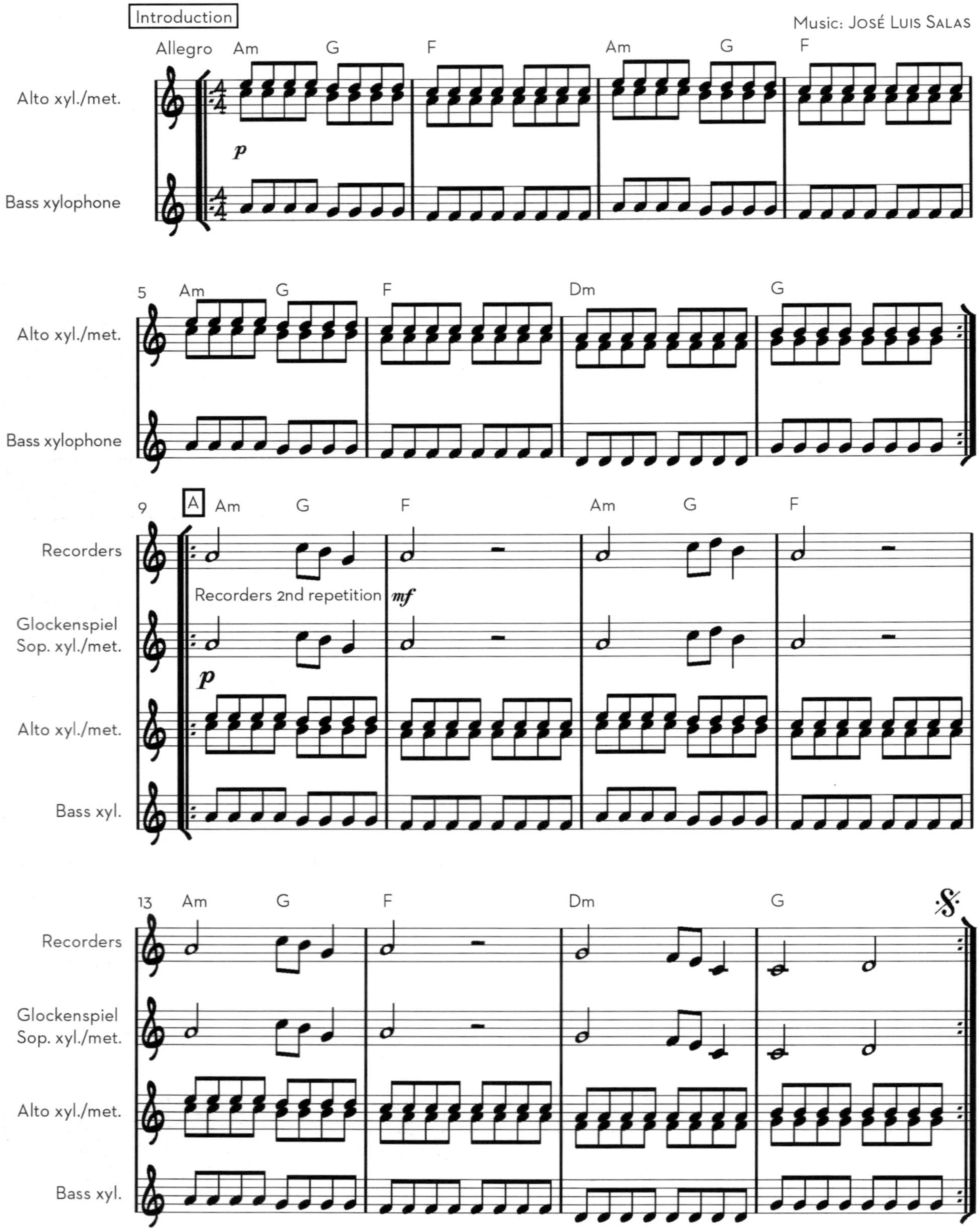

2
17
B
C
Dm
Em
F
G
C
Dm
Recorders
Glockenspiel
Sop. xyl./met.
Alto xyl./met.
Bass xyl.
p
22
Em
F
G
C
Am
G
F
mf
Recorders 2nd repetition
27
Dm
G
Am
G
F

You can accompany this composition with a djembe by playing the following rhythmic *ostinato:*

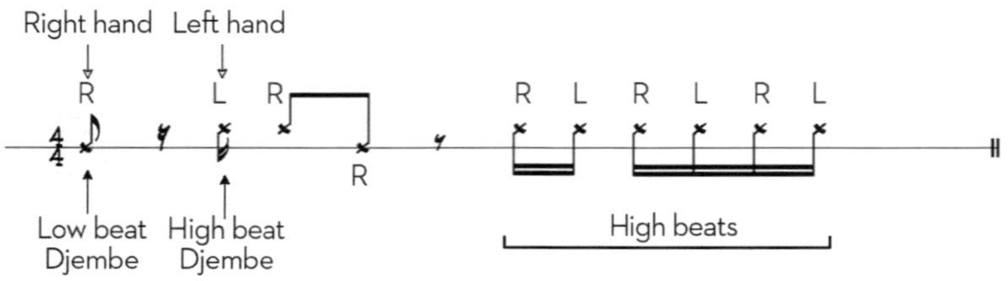

Download and print the worksheet you will find in the OLC to complete the concept map of the unit.

F ... — Set of t ..., c ... and p ... beliefs, connected with a certain g ... area (town, country, region, etc.)

M ... folklore — Traditional music (*s ..., d ... and i ...*)

Our folklore

- **Musical instruments**
  - **S ...** — Examples: *gu ..., lute, b ..., hurdy-gurdy,* Canarian *t ..., rabel, ch ...*
  - **W ...** — Examples: Basque *tx ...*, Catalan *f ...*, Basque *a ..., dulzaina, ch ..., bagpipes,* etc.
  - **P ...** — Examples: *castanets, t ..., cowbells, tamboril, carraca, z ..., arrabel, tx ...*, etc.
- **S ...** — Very diverse themes
  - Ch ... carols
  - C ... ongs
  - W ... songs
  - L ...
  - R ... songs
  - Serenades
  - W ... ongs
  - *Qu* ... songs
  - C ...'s songs
- **Dances** — Some of the most representative are:

M ...	**Galicia**
Z ...	**Basque Country**
J ...	**Navarre and Aragon**
S ...	**Castile-La Mancha**
S ...	**Extremadura**
S ...	**Catalonia**
P ...	**Murcia**
S ...	**Andalusia**
I ...	**Canary Islands**
etc.	

- **Folklore in modern music** — There are new musical t ... in which the melodies, rhythms and instruments of folkloric music are present. These trends are usually called *f ... m ..., w ... music, eth ... music.*

FINAL ACTIVITIES

1. Explain in English what *folklore* is.
2. What different manifestations can we find in musical folklore? Explain in English.
3. What characteristics are common for all types of folkloric or traditional music? Explain in English.
4. Complete the following table in your Workbook with the traditional instruments that seemed the most interesting to you. You can also use another instrument (that was not in the book) if it is typical in your community or region.

Family	Instrument	Origin	Spanish
String	...	...	...
String	...	...	...
Wind	...	...	...
Wind	...	...	...
Percussion	...	...	...
Percussion	...	...	...

5. Name the following folkloric musical instruments, in English and in Spanish.

1

2

3

4

5

6. **Check what you learnt about the folkloric dances in Spain. In your Workbook, write where the following dances are typical:**

Sardana: ___

Zortzico: ___

Jota: ___

Seguidillas: ___

Muñeira: ___

Isa: ___

Sevillanas: ___

Son: ___

Parranda: ___

El uno y el dos: ___

7. **Learn more about the folklore of your community. In groups, look for information about its typical dances, folklore festivals, choirs and dance associations, etc.**

FINAL PROJECT

1. In groups: Make a concept map about the musical folklore in the country your group chooses.
2. Search on different websites to find out information. You have several websites on the complementary material.
3. Download an example of the concept map about folklore in Honduras.
4. You will also have to prepare a list of videos in YouTube to present the subject better to your classmates.

A ICT WORKSHOP: SCORE EDITOR

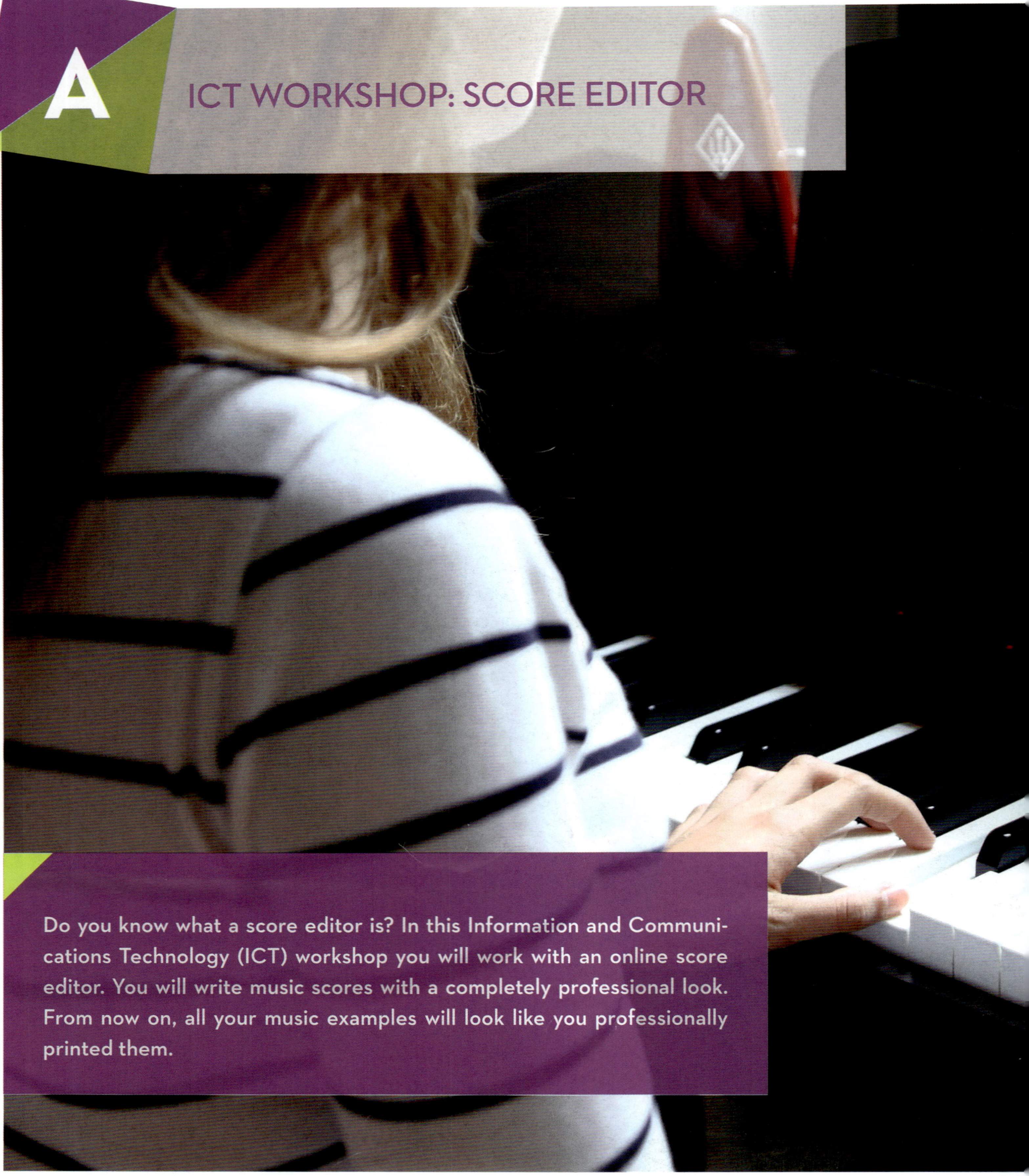

Do you know what a score editor is? In this Information and Communications Technology (ICT) workshop you will work with an online score editor. You will write music scores with a completely professional look. From now on, all your music examples will look like you professionally printed them.

Contents

1 Score Editing with Noteflight

Noteflight is an **online score editor.** This means that you do not need to install any programme on your computer to create and edit music scores. Although the programme is in English, it is very easy to use, so you do not need to worry about the language. Now we will look at what steps to follow to write scores with this simple editor.

1.1. Signing up with Noteflight

To start working with Noteflight you must sign up on the programme's website. You must go to the link http://noteflight.com/login and click on the option ***Sign Up*** (Registrarse). You only need to write your email address and choose a password which you will enter two times.

You will then open your email to active your account. This will allow you to share your scores. You only need to enter a **username** so your classmates can recognise you.

When you have signed up, you can go back to the website and click on ***Log In***. Now we are ready!

1.2. Creating a New Score

To start writing music, click on *New Score*. This will open Noteflight's work environment.

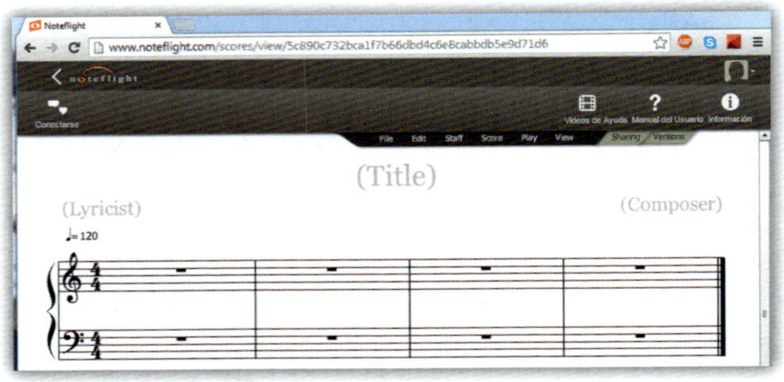

The first thing we will do is **give our score a title,** indicate who the **composer** is and finally, indicate the **tempo.** We will click on each of the text indications (shaded grey) and we will write the following:

a) **Title:**
Twinkle, Twinkle Little Star.
b) **Composer:**
Popular.
c) **Lyricist:**
Allegro.

DID YOU KNOW?

There are professional score editing programmes that allow you to use the programmes for a specific period of time. If you visit the websites of the two editors that are the most popular with professional musicians (Finale and Sibelius), you can download, install and try these programmes on your computer.

WORKSHEET

1. Do you know the meaning of these words?
   - Password
   - Username
   - Sign up
   - Log in
   - Log out
   - Score
   - Editor
   - Tempo

   a) Write them.
   b) Say the translation to your classmate.
   c) Ask him or her.
   d) Swap.

The song we will write only needs one stave. To **delete the lower stave,** double-click on any bar of the lower stave. (It will then appear in colour.) Next press the ***Delete*** button (Supr) on the computer keyboard. The lower stave will disappear.

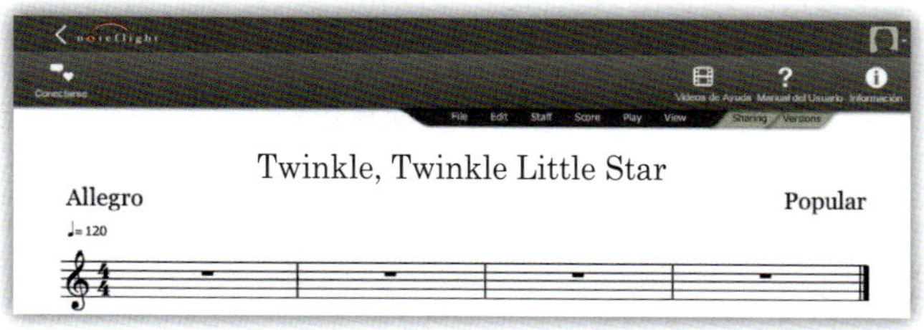

We have eliminated the extra stave. Now we can start to write the song.

1.3. Writing Music with Noteflight (I)

To write music with Noteflight, we must remember the following considerations:

1. **Click on the bar** where you want to write music.
2. When you place the mouse over the bar you have selected, you will see that **a note head appears.** Then click on the note you want to write.
3. Most importantly: we can **select the note value** we want (semibreve, minim, crotchet, etc.) only after clicking on the note we have written.

This is how the first part of the song will look:

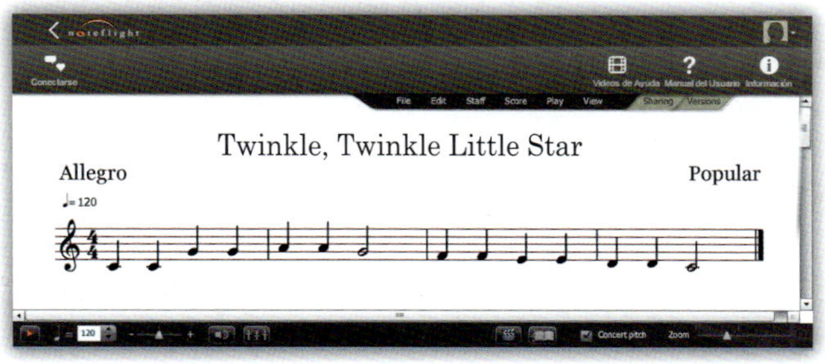

Finally, we will save our score to continue editing it at another time. Go to ***File / Save.*** When we open the programme again, our saved score will be there.

ACTIVITIES

1. Review everything that you have studied up to now by writing the first part of *Twinkle, Twinkle Little Star* in the score editor Noteflight.

REMEMBER

It is important to save your project in Noteflight frequently. Because it is programmed with Flash technology and it is an online programme, there may occasionally be a problem which may lose the work you have done. You will not be able to recover unsaved work.

WORKSHEET

2. Do you know the meaning of these words?
   - Stave / Staff
   - Delete
   - Bar
   - Note head
   - Note value
   - Semibreve
   - Minim
   - Crotchet
   - File
   - Save

   a) Write them.

   b) Say the translation to your classmate.

   c) Ask him or her.

   d) Swap.

1.4. Writing Music with Noteflight (II)

In the score that we wrote you can see that there are only four bars. **To add more bars** you must know about Noteflight's other options. First, place the mouse cursor over the stave. (You can select the last bar, for example.) You will see some symbols that we did not study before:

We can see that at the end of the bar there is a symbol with a **plus sign (+).** If we click on this sign we will see that it adds another bar. We can also click on the **minus sign (–) to eliminate a bar.** To continue writing the song *Twinkle, Twinkle Little Star* we will need 8 more bars. The score will look like what you see below.

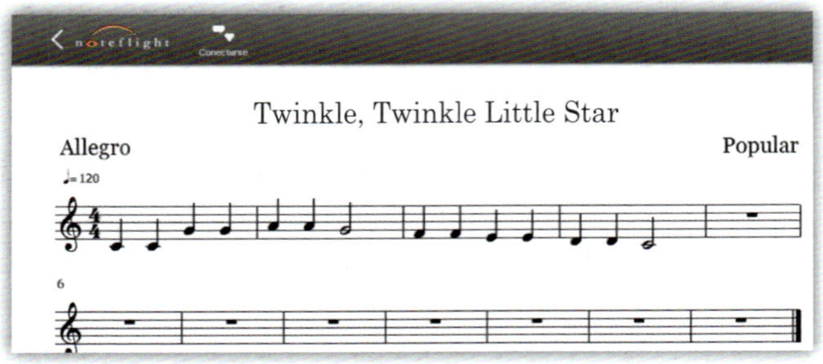

When we have the number of bars that we need to write all the song, we will write the rest of the music.

Now we have our first song written with Noteflight.

DID YOU KNOW?

One of the most common errors made when we start editing music with Noteflight is to confuse the options *Add Bar* and *Add Staff*. (Remember that 'staff' is the American spelling for 'stave'.) The first adds another bar and the second creates an additional instrument.

ACTIVITIES

2. Review everything that you have studied up to now by writing the complete song *Twinkle, Twinkle Little Star* with the score editor Noteflight. Do not forget to save your work.

1.5. Writing Music with Noteflight (III)

Finally, you will see some options that you can use to make your scores better: different types of lines, repeat signs, how to include lyrics in the music, etc.

We will continue using *Twinkle, Twinkle Little Star* for our work. The first part of the song repeats, so we will need **to put an end repeat sign** in the score. You must click on the bar line where you want to put the repeat sign. A series of options will appear under the stave.

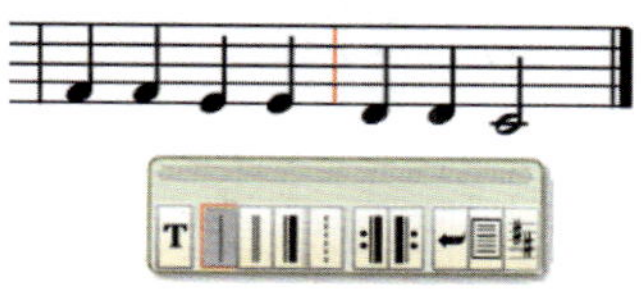

You can see that the line you clicked on turns red and some **bar line options** appear under the stave. Select the end repeat sign option. The score will look like this:

Next we will look at **how to indicate dynamics or intensities.** To indicate that after a certain note we want the intensity to be, for example, soft or *piano*, we will click on that note and the following window will open:

Click on the symbol *f*, and it will create a space under the note so you can indicate the intensity that you want. The example will look like this:

WORKSHEET

3. Do you know the meaning of these words?
   - Repeat sign
   - Lyrics
   - End repeat sign
   - Click on
   - Turns red
   - Bar line options
   - Ties
   - Dynamic markings

   a) Write them.

   b) Say the translation to your classmate.

   c) Ask him or her.

   d) Swap.

REMEMBER

The most common musical intensities are:

pp = *Pianissimo* (very soft).

p = *Piano* (soft).

mf = *Mezzoforte* (moderately loud).

f = *Forte* (loud).

ff = *Fortissimo* (very loud).

For gradual increases and decreases in intensity, we use the regulators or indications 'crescendo' and 'diminuendo'. Noteflight considers these intensity **regulators 'lines'** (see the next page).

So if we want to use some of the most common lines in music (ties, dynamic markings like *crescendo* and *diminuendo*, etc.), we will click on a bar and the options window will appear. Now we will click on the *crescendo* symbol.

When we click on the *crescendo* symbol, some options appear. These options are for inserting lines in scores.

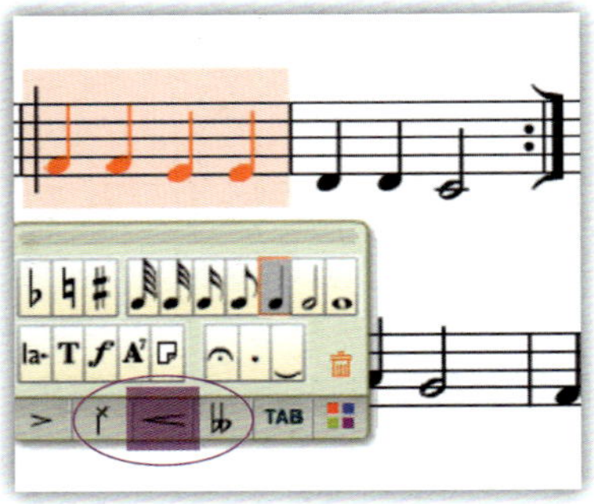

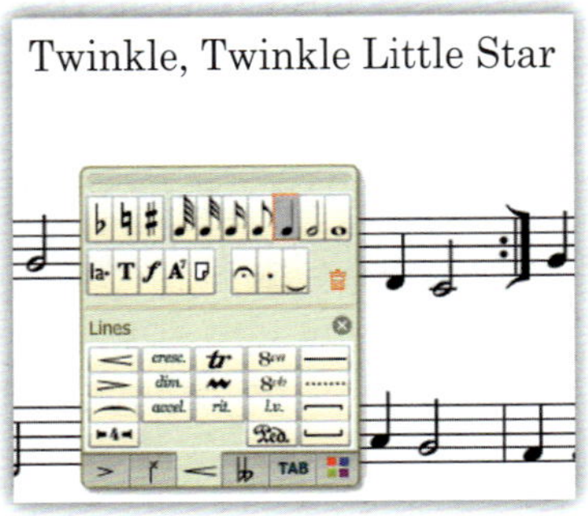

We can see the *Lines* menu in the image above. Now we only have to select the one we want and it will be placed automatically on the note that we selected previously, as you can see in the following image.

Next we will learn **how to put in some lyrics.** We will click on the first note where the lyrics start. The same window appears and we can see an option represented with the syllable ***la.***

When we click on option *la*, the cursor will blink so we can start to write the lyrics to the song. We must remember that when a word has several syllables, these must be separated by a hyphen (on the computer keyboard). **To separate a word from another,** we will use the computer keyboard space bar. Here is an example of the beginning of the song:

WORKSHEET

4. Do you know the meaning of these words?
   - Bar line options
   - Ties
   - Dynamic markings
   - Blink
   - Hyphen
   - Computer keyboard space bar

   a) Write them.

   b) Say the translation to your classmate.

   c) Ask him or her.

   d) Swap.

Finally, we will learn **to 'format' the score.** This means that we will distribute the bars on the staff so that they are not too close together. Imagine that we want the song *Twinkle, Twinkle Little Star* to change to a different stave every four bars. We will click on the first bar we want to format. Without releasing the left mouse button, drag to the last bar you want to format. You will see that the bars selected change colour. With the bars selected, go to *Score / System Break*, and the four bars we selected will be on only one stave, as you can see below.

REMEMBER

When you work with music technology it is recommended that you know some basic terms of the programmes you use. These are normally in English. So, 'score' means *'partitura'* and 'system break' means *'salto de sistema'* or *'salto de pentagrama'*.

ACTIVITIES

3. Write the following score to review everything that we studied in this score editor workshop.

WORKSHEET

5. Do you know the meaning of these words?
   - Format
   - Without releasing
   - Drag to
   - System break

   a) Write them.

   b) Say the translation to your classmate.

   c) Ask him or her.

   d) Swap.

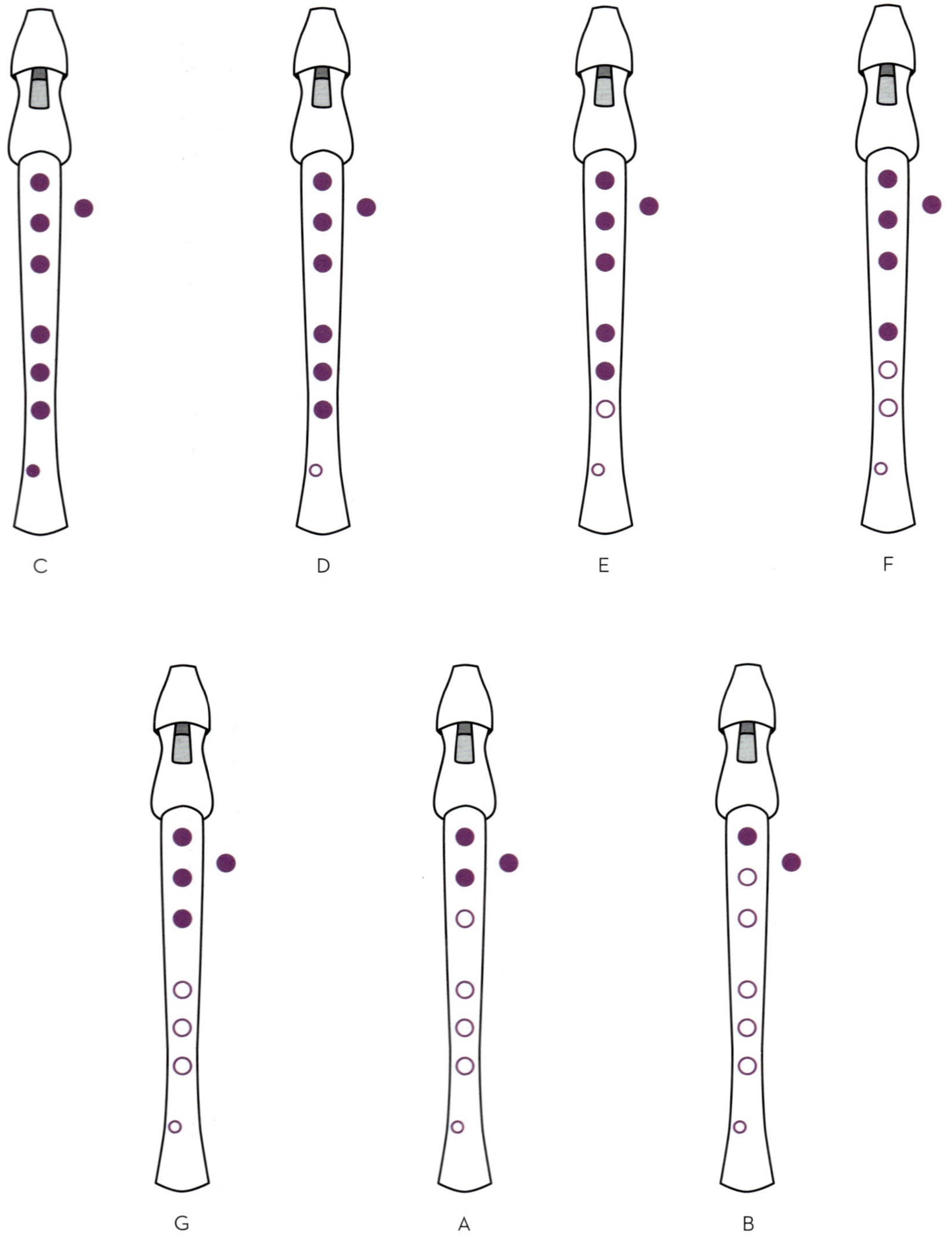
C
D
E
F
G
A
B

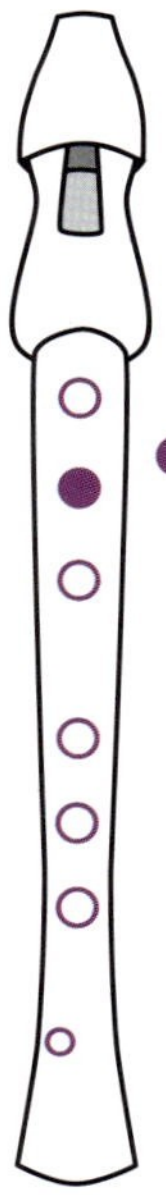

C

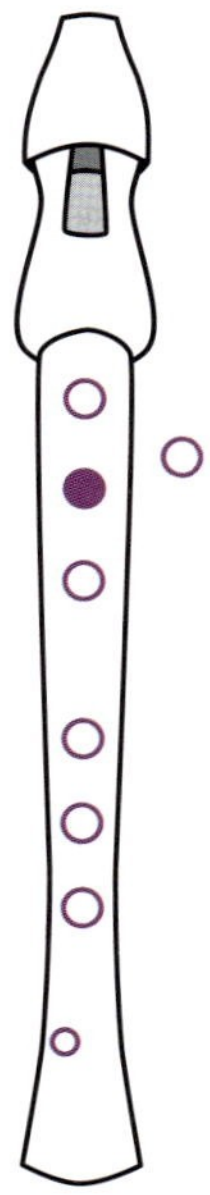

D

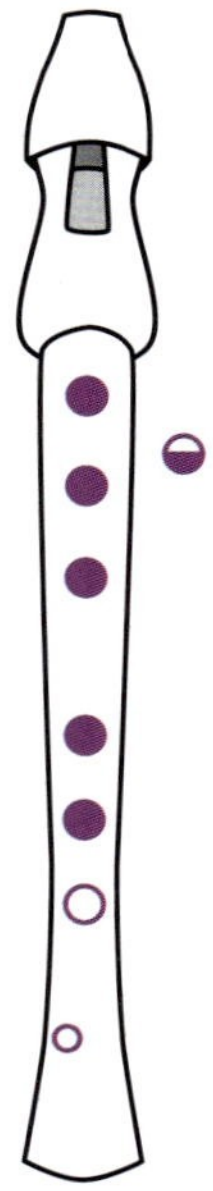

E

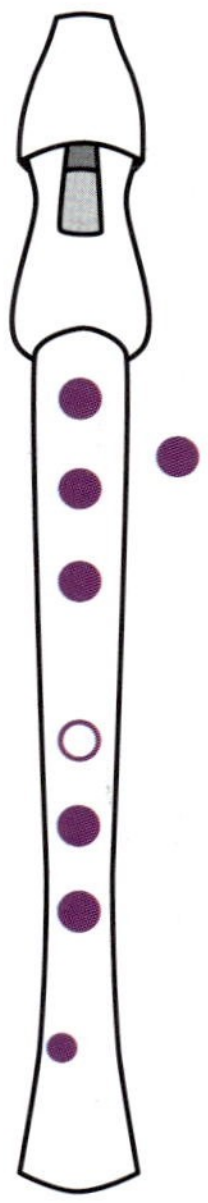

F♯

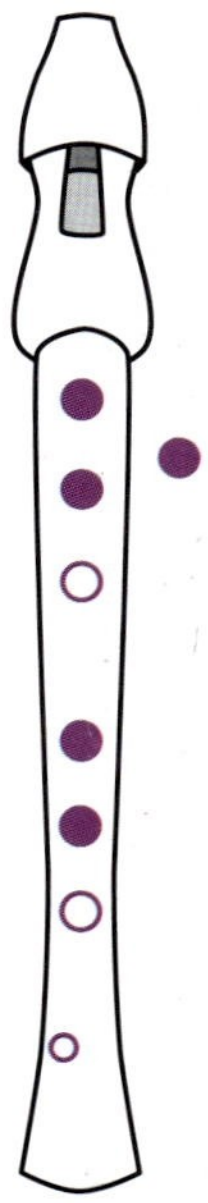

G♯

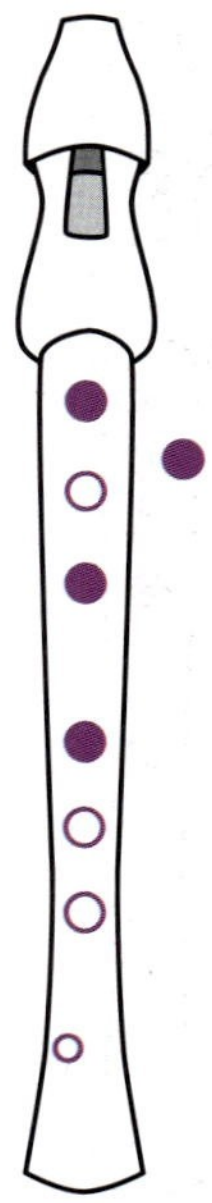

B♭